T0268331

FEELING AT HOME

FEELING AT HOME

Transforming the Politics of Housing

Alva Gotby

VERSO
London • New York

First published by Verso 2025
© Alva Gotby 2025

All rights reserved

The moral rights of the author have been asserted

1 3 5 7 9 10 8 6 4 2

Verso
UK: 6 Meard Street, London W1F 0EG
US: 207 East 32nd Street, New York, NY 10016
versobooks.com

Verso is the imprint of New Left Books

ISBN-13: 978-1-80429-621-9
ISBN-13: 978-1-80429-664-6 (US EBK)
ISBN-13: 978-1-80429-663-9 (UK EBK)

British Library Cataloguing in Publication Data
A catalogue record for this book is available from the British Library

Library of Congress Cataloging-in-Publication Data

Names: Gotby, Alva, author.
Title: Feeling at home : transforming the politics of housing / Alva Gotby.

Description: London ; Brooklyn, N.Y. : Verso Books, 2025. | Includes bibliographical references.
Identifiers: LCCN 2024031911 (print) | LCCN 2024031912 (ebook) | ISBN 9781804296219 (hardback) | ISBN 9781804296646 (ebk)
Subjects: LCSH: Housing policy--Great Britain. | Housing--Great Britain. | Home ownership--Social aspects--Great Britain.
Classification: LCC HD7333.A3 G66 2025 (print) | LCC HD7333.A3 (ebook) | DDC 363.50941--dc23/eng/20241011
LC record available at https://lccn.loc.gov/2024031911
LC ebook record available at https://lccn.loc.gov/2024031912

Typeset in Garamond by Biblichor Ltd, Scotland
Printed and bound by CPI Group (UK) Ltd, Croydon CR0 4YY

Contents

Introduction

Housing Matters

Housing is at the heart of much of our lives. It is where we rest, eat, relax. Having a home is essential for our long-term survival, as well as our day-to-day wellbeing. Without a stable home, people tend to experience mental and physical health issues, and often premature death. Housing, therefore, is at the core of social reproduction – all the things that go into ensuring the relative wellbeing of people, enabling them to go about their lives and go to work. Housing also has a central role in ideologies about what it means to live a good and dignified life. Those without stable housing are regarded as discardable, while those who have access to good, desirable housing are often seen as having made it; having made good and responsible decisions for which the home is both a sign and a reward. Moreover, having a home is often linked to ideologies of family – the idealised group of legally and biologically linked people who are seen as the natural inhabitants of the home.

But decent housing is becoming harder than ever to access. From 2021 to the time of writing in 2024, rent increases in cities like London and Manchester have far outstripped inflation, and more and more renters are no longer able to afford somewhere to live. In the last months of 2022, the number of people in London sleeping rough for the first time went up by 29 per cent.[1] What has long been known as a housing crisis is now affecting an ever-increasing number of people. This is in many ways an unusual moment. But at the same time, this crisis of affordability is nothing unexpected. The UK housing system has long been at the centre of the national economy, creating pressure on successive governments to maintain house prices at all costs, and ensure the profitability of the private rented sector. And across the world, many local but interlinked crises of housing affordability are unfolding, leading to precarity and homelessness for ever larger groups of people.

As the crisis unfolds, we are also witnessing the revival of housing organising, both in the UK and internationally. This movement has been regaining strength after the 2008 global financial crisis. The collapse of the sub-prime mortgage market in the US grew into a general financial crisis, the reverberations of which were also felt most acutely in the housing sector. In Spain, homeowners – whose homes were mortgaged and therefore actually owned by the banks – got organised to resist foreclosures. In Germany, Ireland, the UK, the US and many other countries, renters have started to organise against their exploitation by landlords. Internationally, people are resisting global corporate landlords such as Blackstone, which are increasingly buying up devalued housing stock as an investment.[2]

In the UK, however, the rental market is dominated by small landlords, who tend to own one or two properties to let. Housing policy since the 1980s has facilitated a fundamental shift from a rental sector mainly consisting of council-owned housing – which had secure tenancies and rent control – to domination by a deregulated private rented sector. This sector is characterised by high rents, short-term contracts, and poor housing conditions. It was set up with the sole purpose of making landlordism a profitable investment. Buy-to-let mortgages were introduced in 1996 to make it easier for individuals to become landlords. In England since the early 2000s, the size of the private rented sector has doubled, and 82 per cent of landlords own fewer than five homes.[3] The UK's landlords are not professionals or big corporations. Being a landlord was sold to individuals as a secure investment – people will always need homes – and one that requires very little work on the part of the landlord. The abolition of rent controls in 1988 meant that landlords could set whatever rent they wanted, and poor enforcement of tenants' legal rights to decent standards has meant that landlords can often get away with not paying for even the most basic and essential repairs. The tenants who complain about high rents or low standards can easily be evicted. There has also been a shift towards a culture in which private tenants have come to accept poor housing conditions, living in fear they might lose their home if they ask for too much.

While councils and housing associations combined still house about 16 per cent of all households in England,[4] the more secure tenure forms that social housing offer have been 'residualised' – treated as a form of housing suitable only for the poorest people, who can't afford to either buy or rent privately. Social housing has become almost impossible to access, as housing waiting lists have swelled and councils have to reserve their local stock for rehousing the most vulnerable residents who have become homeless. Decades of underinvestment in social housing has led to a decline in housing stock quality, and social housing estates have been demonised as the cause of poverty, criminality, and 'antisocial behaviour'.[5] The housing association sector is increasingly reliant on private sector finance, and thus increasingly acting according to the same logic as corporate landlords.

There is currently broad agreement that we are living through a housing crisis, and commentators from across the political spectrum are calling for urgent action. But accounts of this crisis tend to disagree on its causes as well as its solutions. There is a familiar story circulating in the housing movement today, about how housing is becoming increasingly financialised – treated as an asset to make profit from, rather than homes for people to live in. This story makes a lot of sense, especially in countries such as the US, where large corporate landlords increasingly dominate housing provision. But, as Susanne Soederberg has pointed out, the financialisation narrative tends to neglect the fact that profits from housing derive from working-class tenants' ability to pay their rent. The concept of financialisation, she argues, can obscure the links between housing and the sphere of production, in which tenants are workers, and instead focus too much on the financial sector. Soederberg uses the term 'secondary exploitation' to highlight the centrality of rent extraction in capitalist economies without losing sight of the fact that this extraction is dependent on exploitation of workers by capitalists.[6] In a similar vein, Nick Bano has criticised the discourse which locates the cause of the housing crisis in foreign investors profiting from a 'housing bubble'. Housing, he writes, has become so profitable because working-class people are forced to hand over increasingly exorbitant rents in order to access shelter. The state also underwrites this system through housing benefits – massive subsidies to landlords which serve to shore up the profitability of landlordism and therefore the stability of the housing system as a whole.[7] The profitability of housing as investment thus depends on the exploitation of the working class and large amounts of public money.

We need to keep this circuit in mind in order to understand the role of housing under capitalism, not only as a space for financial investors to make money but crucially also as a site for the reproduction of labour power. The story of the financialisation of housing often relies on a notion that the pre-financialised, pre-neoliberal housing system was better at meeting people's needs for housing, and that housing under the 'golden age' of post-war capitalism was decommodified and therefore less capitalist. Explicitly or implicitly, this argument states that we can resolve the housing crisis by returning to this system.[8] This narrative has some truth to it, but it is at best a partial understanding of housing under capitalism. The housing system as we know it today is incredibly harmful and exploitative. In some ways it marks a return to the housing system that existed before public housing was created in many European countries in the early twentieth century. So maybe we could demand that the state does again what it did then: build massive amounts of public housing?

But in many ways, our situation today is drastically different from that of the first half of the twentieth century. The UK today actually has a larger housing stock, despite catastrophist accounts of a desperate housing shortage. There are 1.1 million vacant homes in England alone, and across England and Wales, 70 per cent of all homes are underoccupied.[9] A lot of the housing stock is in poor condition, but most of it could be improved, and much more cheaply than if we were to demolish it and build new housing. Today, there isn't a shortage in the absolute number of houses, or in the ratio of homes per household.[10] Liberals (and many on the left as well) like to talk about how building more will solve the housing crisis, as if the high prices of housing were just the result of an imbalance of supply and demand. The social democratic response is to concede that we need more housing, but that it should be social housing, or at least 'affordable' housing.[11]

But the building industry takes a big toll on the climate, as concrete is a considerable source of CO_2 emissions. If the UK government were to meet its target of building 300,000 homes a year, housing alone would account for 104 per cent of the UK's total 'climate budget' by 2050 – the amount of emissions the country allows itself across all sectors of the economy in order to have a 50 per cent chance of avoiding climate catastrophe.[12] If we were to apply more stringent requirements on emissions, we would basically have to stop building new properties and spend all available resources on insulating existing homes. But that doesn't sound very appealing as a policy, especially not to the developer lobby, which is a powerful influence in UK politics.

If we can't build ourselves out of the housing crisis, we could turn existing privately owned homes to public ownership. This is a much better approach, because it would involve taking houses from the private rented sector and turning them into homes that are actually available for the working class, at the same time as minimising the exploitation of that class within the housing sector. It would work to counter gentrification in many cities, a phenomenon largely driven by unaffordable private rents forcing people to move out of the communities where they have lived for decades. This is a kind of reverse Right to Buy – the policy introduced by the Thatcher government which meant that people could buy their council homes. It is an oft-repeated fact in the UK housing movement that over 40 per cent of the housing sold through Right to Buy made its way into the hands of private landlords.[13] Even better than buying back homes, we could simply expropriate private landlords – the parasites who thrive upon the impoverishment of workers and surplus populations. This would challenge one central front of capitalist accumulation today. However, it doesn't go far enough.

The idea that we can just return to a pre-neoliberal, pre-Thatcher housing system – taking back the housing stock that has been lost through Right to Buy – is often premised on a nostalgia for the welfare state that conveniently ignores the many issues with council housing as it existed in the mid-twentieth century. It's all well and good to insist on an expansion in the council-owned housing stock, and a simultaneous reinvestment in improving the conditions of the existing stock to compensate for decades of disinvestment and declining standards. But in itself, the emphasis on expanding the stock of council-owned properties risks missing the fact that our demands should be focused not just on the number of homes, or even the number of homes of a particular type of tenancy, but more fundamentally what those homes look like, and what types of lives they enable.

The main issue with arguments about housing on the left today is that they mainly consider housing from legal and economic perspectives: what types of tenure are available, and how much housing costs. While these perspectives are essential, they tend to get stuck in the same debates about forms of housing that have been repeated for over a century. A return to council-owned housing can thus be portrayed as a solution to the housing crisis. 'Build more council housing' emerges as a magic fix to the crisis, without much discussion of what that housing looks like, or how and where it has been built.

The slogan that housing is treated as assets rather than homes ignores the fact that homes, too, have an important role in shaping capitalist social relations. Housing should be a use value, not an exchange value, we are told. But this displays a rather poor understanding of these Marxist categories. All commodities have a use value as well as an exchange value. No one would buy a useless thing. But what a thing is used for may vary, and the same object can have a range of different uses. This book looks at the different uses of housing under capitalism – from an asset that reinforces family ties by storing value for future generations, to a space for the regeneration of labour power and domestic labour (so that people can continue going to work), to a place where social stratifications based on gender, race, disability, and class are constituted and reproduced. Rather than repeating the claim that homes should be a use value and not an exchange value, we need to ask ourselves: a use value *for what*?

The housing movement has been so focused on the types of tenure we want that we have left unexplored questions of what people do in their homes, and what function the home has under capitalism. In short, it has neglected the issue of housing as a site of social reproduction of the proletariat. This focus on the legal and economic aspects of housing has also led to an at best partial understanding of *why* housing matters as a site of struggle under capital. Housing is in fact not only an investment vehicle for landlords and homeowners. Its core function is still as home – that is, as a key site of social reproduction. If it wasn't something we all need to survive and live at least minimally decent lives, it wouldn't also be such a lucrative investment. Like all commodities, housing is always use value and exchange value at the same time. The project of this book is to take housing seriously as an aspect of capitalist social reproduction, rather than merely mourning the supposed commodification of housing under neoliberal capitalism.

Profit-Making and Class Struggle

Housing politics defines people's daily existence, and in various ways it affects everyone. This broad relevance of housing as a political issue makes it a fertile ground for organising. Yet the left has traditionally centred its organising efforts on the workplace, bracketing housing as a relatively marginal matter. This line of thinking has followed Friedrich Engels' assertion that poor housing conditions are a secondary evil under capitalism.[14] It is in the workplace, the argument goes, that the working class can directly interrupt the flow of capital and its production of value. But much has changed since the heyday of working-class trade unionism. Work in Europe and North America has become increasingly precarious, and people often lack stable and long-term employment, which makes it harder to use strikes and other tactics that would interrupt the production of surplus value. Layers of outsourcing often make it difficult to determine exactly who the target of a strike should be. The fact that a large part of the workforce are now engaged in reproductive work such as healthcare and education, where the refusal of that labour might harm those cared for, means that many workers are more reluctant to take strike action. The wave of strikes in 2022 shows that strike action is not impossible, and remains a powerful tool for working-class power. But strikes seem to have lost their status as *the* essential tactic for working-class struggle.

According to one reading of this shift, the economy has also changed to a degree where industrial capitalism is no longer primary to the economy, and we have instead entered a phase of rentier capitalism. This form of capitalism derives value from the ownership and monopoly control of (physical or intellectual) assets rather than the production of goods and services.[15] Housing and other asset classes emerge as a key economical factor because they are a source of rent. According to this argument, then, housing was once secondary to industrial production, but has now become primary. And, at the same time, housing struggles have become a primary site of struggle. Neil Gray writes:

> Engels' thesis had validity in the 1870s, and arguably much of the twentieth century, when considered in relation to the emergence of a powerful workers' movement within industry and manufacturing. But in a period in Britain

> and Ireland marked by industrial decomposition, a resurgent rentier economy . . . and the increasing centrality of housing to respective national political economies and the structures of capitalism, the housing question must be reconsidered.[16]

But in the same essay, Gray makes the compelling argument that people struggle on the sites where they encounter the capitalist drive to accumulate in their own lives.[17] For the large portion of the proletariat that was never part of the industrial working class, this has often been in housing. Gray uses the groundbreaking 1915 Glasgow rent strike as an example of this: direct action targeting the profit-making ability of private landlords, whose core protagonists were largely working-class housewives. These women encountered capitalism in the form of profit-hungry private landlords, who derived large amounts of money from cramming working-class renters into overcrowded and poorly maintained tenements, increasing the rent when they saw fit to do so. The organised action by people who had previously been dismissed as unimportant to the working-class struggle successfully forced the UK government to impose rent controls, which were in place in one form or another for over seventy years.

This action in fact forced a shift in the UK economy, ensuring that being a private landlord wouldn't be a profitable enterprise, and secured the working class access to more affordable housing for decades. Rather than only thinking of class struggle as something that changes in response to shifting forms of capitalist accumulation, then, we can consider how forms of struggle make particular forms of extraction and exploitation more or less attractive to the capitalist class. Put differently, we can think of both 'productive' and 'reproductive' aspects of the economy as potential arenas of class struggle, where the capitalist class and the working class will be able to impose their terms in accordance with the relative strength of that class in a particular area. So, in a way, it might not be so much that the working class naturally had more power in the space of the workplace compared with that of the domestic sphere. Rather, decades of organising meant that the working class had built more power in the factories than in the home. This could have been different, if different priorities had been established. And productive and reproductive spheres are never fully distinct: housing is clearly a sphere of both production (house-building and maintenance) and reproduction (a space where capitalists can extract profit because people have a need for shelter to be able to survive and meet their other needs). Today, as more and more people carry out their wage work at home, the distinction between productive and reproductive spheres is again becoming increasingly blurry.

So the argument that housing matters now because of a shift in the economy towards more extractive (rather than exploitative) practices of profit-making might understate the role that this form of capitalism has long had in many people's lives, especially women, who have typically been designated the people responsible for reproduction more than wage work. The working class come across capital in many different forms, and it's only by attacking capital from all sides that we have a realistic chance of bringing it down.[18] So rather than an understanding of capitalism, and therefore also working-class struggle, shifting from a primacy of industrial sphere to a primacy of rent extraction, we can see these as interconnected parts that have all always mattered in anti-capitalist struggle. The fact that landlords (private and public) have been able to insert themselves between people and their need for housing is a fundamental condition of capitalist economies, where the things people need to survive have been made conditional on paying for them. As Søren Mau puts it, 'an understanding of class as a shared relation to the means of social reproduction . . . allows us to broaden our notion of class struggle and see how struggles across the entire social field can be part of the same political project: wrenching the conditions of life from the grip of capital'.[19] This perspective helps us see the role of housing struggle within a broader field of the constitution of capitalism: it was partly because a women-led housing movement won a big victory at the start of the twentieth century that housing became a less important site for profit-making.

This also speaks to the potential of a wide set of proletarian movements working in conjunction (though not necessarily formal coalition) with each other as a way of challenging capital from all sides. If we attack profit-making from many different points, we make it harder for capital to move around and find new avenues for investment should it encounter resistance in one sphere. This would also enable a fuller understanding of working-class composition, as the proletariat consists of many different groups that often have different positions vis-à-vis capital. Large parts of the proletariat have been excluded from wage work, but still encounter many forms of capital extraction and exploitation in their lives.

Workers who have been marked as less productive because of various forms of disability or illness have been forced to subsist on benefits, because they are seen as a 'cost' to employers and therefore not employable.[20] As Beatrice Adler-Bolton and Artie Vierkant point out, however, these workers are subjected to forms of 'extractive abandonment', through which their very exclusion from waged work is turned into a source of profit. The forms of care to which the medical, pharmaceutical, and 'supported accommodation' industries subject the disabled and sick are very profitable business indeed.[21] Migrants are often relegated to precarious, informal, and unattractive forms of work, outside of the sphere of industrial production. Women have historically been seen as unwaged reproductive labourers first and foremost, and only part of the workforce under particular circumstances. It is only by recognising these different forms of capitalist exploitation that we can begin to challenge capital as a whole. In order to fully do justice to the housing question, we need to assert that the reproduction of the working class has always been central to capitalist economies.

Social Reproduction and Domesticity

Despite housing being a core reproductive concern, the topic of social reproduction hasn't been very visible in housing struggles. Gender, too, has been marginalised within contemporary debates on housing, regardless of the prominent role women have had in struggles for better housing. Indeed, feminist concerns regarding what housing is currently used for, and what it could become, are typically bracketed in a movement focused narrowly on the economic and legal aspects of housing. This means that housing as a site of domestic violence and reproductive labour tends to disappear, and the demand for more council housing comes to overshadow more radical remakings of the domestic sphere. Put differently, the housing movement has often failed to deal adequately with political questions of *domesticity*.

Housing is a container for many aspects of social reproduction. Home is often where we eat our meals, where children receive much of their early socialisation and education, where many sick, elderly, and disabled people are cared for, where our emotional needs are met, where we rest, and where our health can either be improved or diminished, depending on our housing conditions. What housing looks like will also play a part in shaping the relationships, labours, and outcomes of social reproduction more broadly. While we tend to think of both 'care' and 'home' as inherently good things, they are central to the continual reproduction of capitalism. As such, they are also imbued with reactionary ideology. Alison Blunt and Robyn Dowling write that a 'house environment may be alienating and oppressive as easily as it may be supportive and comfortable'.[22] I want to add that even those home environments that are genuinely supportive may in many cases be premised on exploitative divisions of reproductive labour. A task of this book is to interrogate the various ways in which conservative social values shape how we view home and housing. As Susan Fraiman suggests, domesticity is not inherently conservative, and some critiques by the left of the domestic sphere are implicitly misogynistic in their quick dismissals of both domesticity and its attendant femininity.[23] But we need to identify conservative elements in order to move towards a more liberatory version of domesticity.

Dominant social relations are literally built into our homes. For example, many modern kitchens were designed with the assumption that a lone woman would be working in that space.[24] This doesn't mean that housing design is a determining factor for all of social reproduction and its attendant relations of labour. As the feminist architecture collective Matrix points out, buildings 'reflect dominant values in our society, political and architectural views, people's demands and the constraints of finance, but we can live in them in different ways from those originally intended'.[25] People tend to make use of the space they have access to in ways that support their household in the best possible way. But domestic space isn't endlessly malleable, and domestic design tends to reflect normative assumptions about what households should look like and how they should use their home. Thus, it encourages the reproduction of a particular form of household – typically the ideal of a heteronormative, two-parent nuclear family living together in a one-family home.

The feminist slogan 'the personal is political' might be usefully repurposed to understand why housing matters. This phrase can help us understand how mundane domestic realities are often essential for shaping people's political subjectivity – the way they relate to social and material aspects of the world, their expectations in life, and their relationship to other people. The interaction of productive and reproductive spheres, of work and home, means that housing struggles should always play a central role in working-class struggles more broadly. Moreover, the housing movement shouldn't ignore the question of how people use their homes, and demand homes that are actually part of the abolition of domination both in formal workplaces and at home. It is when we begin to acknowledge this interaction and challenge the way housing is organised as part of capitalist reproduction that we can also begin to demand homes that are different; that do not only satisfy people's need for shelter under capitalism but could form a basis for radically rethinking our lives.

This book explores the symptoms of a housing system fundamentally unable to meet most people's need for good housing. In some of the essays in this book, I look at some of the most common issues that people experience, such as frequent evictions and poor-quality housing. While my examples are often from the UK, this book is an attempt to understand aspects of housing under capitalism more broadly, and many of the political and theoretical issues raised here are also relevant to other countries in Europe and North America. I also present a critique of common solutions to the current system – specifically the idea that we can and should return to the forms of housing provision that dominated the twentieth century. I highlight the need for a more visionary politics of housing, which not only aims for a home for everyone, but fundamentally seeks to reshape how housing interacts with other areas of our lives. Against a notion of the ideal home as a private, securitised one-family house that offers a refuge from the public sphere, I make the case for a vision in which home is open, collective, and integrated in the broader social world.

While working on this book, I was also engaged in housing struggles in London. I have learnt about the housing system from other organisers and activists, and have in turn passed on those learnings to others. This book, then, is indebted to conversations taking place within the housing movement today. My analysis is also deeply shaped by the day-to-day work of supporting other renters to challenge landlords, local government, and letting agents, and our collective struggle for better housing for all of us. I hope this book can provide some ideas for expanding that struggle.

1

No Return to Normal

It is hard to deny that we are facing a crisis of evictions and homelessness. During the Covid pandemic, many governments attempted to mitigate this crisis by introducing temporary protections against evictions. This meant that people were able to stay in their homes for a long period of time after receiving an eviction notice – especially if they waited for their landlord to take them to court, which can be a lengthy process. This small victory would not have been possible without the joint effort of the housing movement and its allies. Together, housing organisations in the UK forced the government to put some measures in place to protect renters, despite long-standing Tory loyalty to landlord lobby organisations such as the National Residential Landlords Association.

While we should celebrate these victories, they were temporary solutions which didn't address the causes of evictions and homelessness. Renters have few legal rights, and an extension of the eviction notice period will do nothing to solve this underlying problem. Perhaps more significantly, the imbalance of power between landlords and renters means that many eviction cases won't go to a possession hearing or even be based on a valid eviction notice – many renters simply leave when their landlord tells them to. Landlords often rely on harassment and intimidation if their tenants don't leave, which is illegal but often difficult to prove. Police tend to help landlords evict their tenants illegally, perhaps instinctively acting as the protectors of private property even when the law is on the side of tenants.

This means that until the UK government takes unprecedented measures to protect renters, undoing the legacy of all governments since at least the 1980s, many renters will be forced to leave their homes. The increased danger of evictions and homelessness during the first phase of the Covid pandemic was but a symptom of several deeper crises – a public health crisis, an economic crisis, and a pre-existing housing crisis. We might even begin to question the validity of the language of 'crisis' when the so-called housing crisis is a more or less permanent condition, one that has marked working-class lives for decades. The term 'crisis', while helpful in instilling a sense of political urgency, inevitably gestures towards a moment before the crisis – a time of normalcy. In the imagination of most of the left, that time was the moment before neoliberalism and austerity, when the state took responsibility for attending to people's housing needs. While there is some truth to this account, we cannot let the framing of 'crisis' lead us to a politics which simply demands a return to pre-crisis normalcy. Such politics can't address the fact that housing politics, and welfare politics more broadly, have always been built on very limited ideas of what constitutes 'good-enough' homes for the working class, as well as a specific understanding of what constitutes a 'good' domestic life.

It's more useful to consider all these crises as expressions of underlying contradictions of capitalism, and in particular the contradiction of social reproduction – the processes through which the working class survives and ensures its own replacement through new generations of workers. Capitalist society relies on the existence of relatively (physically and mentally) healthy workers, where 'health' equals the ability to perform a job at an average standard. Yet the imperatives of capitalist accumulation also push against this, by routinely placing the wages of many workers below subsistence levels and resisting the funding of reproductive services and resources through taxation on profits.

A home is supposedly where we rest and restore our capacity to work. Housing is of great importance for the ability of the proletariat to reproduce itself, and therefore for the continued existence of capitalism itself. When in the nineteenth century the British working class became almost incapable of reproducing itself, this was not only because of the conditions of overwork that Karl Marx details in *Capital*, but also because of the extreme conditions in which they were housed. In the slums, malnutrition, contagious diseases, and the lack of adequate sanitation led to high levels of infant mortality as well as a very low life expectancy for those who survived childhood.

The crisis was temporarily resolved towards the end of the nineteenth century and the first half of the twentieth century, through slum clearance and the creation of the working-class housewife. This shift was partly made possible through bourgeois philanthropy, which aimed to replace slums with more respectable housing and simultaneously impose new norms around health, sexuality, and domestic labour. The increasingly private working-class home became a site of reproductive, feminised labour separated from the sphere of production. In middle- and upper-class homes, working-class servants performed the work of reproduction, while bourgeois housewives were responsible for the ethical and spiritual guidance of their husbands and children. The modern notion of home has always been a site for the exploitation of servant labour, often both feminised and racialised. Today we can see this in the employment of live-in carers and nannies – often migrants who suffer extremely low pay and overwork as well as sexual, emotional, and physical abuse. The bourgeois construction of the domestic sphere – as a haven in a heartless world – serves to obscure these forms of exploitation.

The contradiction of reproduction under capitalism was thus 'solved' through the devaluation of feminised reproductive labour, especially when performed by working-class and/or racialised women. In the twentieth century, the creation of the welfare state supplemented the labours of the private household through sectors such as education and healthcare. The welfare state employed many working-class, migrant, and black and brown women to perform draining and low-paid forms of reproductive labour within eldercare, childcare, and healthcare, while middle-class white women later found employment in more professionalised and managerial positions within the same sectors.

The household has always been reliant on the labour of others in order to survive – whether those others be servants, neighbours, relatives, friends, nannies, or public sector workers. And yet the home appears to be an intensely private place. Successive British governments throughout most of the twentieth century were committed to building homes for the working class – all of which were based on a particular vision of what family and reproductive labour should look like.

We are now in a moment where these forms of housing and family have become increasingly insecure. Council homes have been sold off, and younger people can't afford to buy homes; they often can't afford to start families either, particularly in the larger cities. And yet, this political moment continues to rely on ideological notions of the home and the family as the sites of care. As Sophie Lewis has noted, the Covid pandemic served to reprivatise the household through the imperative to stay at home. The family appears to be the natural unit of care and the world outside the house seems threatening, while the private household appears to be 'the prime location of security in our societies'. But, as Lewis insists, the home isn't a safe place.[1] Other than being a site of the exploitation of reproductive labour, it is also a very violent place for many, who suffer physical, psychological, and sexual violence at the hands of their family members. The Covid crisis led to an increase in domestic violence, often aimed at those who have been made responsible for attending to the needs of others. Queer and trans people are also vulnerable to the violence of the heterosexist nuclear family. Moreover, the idealised notion of the family serves to stigmatise many people, especially migrants and people of colour, who have been systematically excluded from the white, bourgeois ideal of domesticity.

This model of the family is closely tied to private property, and especially homeownership. A home is something to aspire to, something to buy in order to start a family. Owning a home, preferably a suburban one-family house, is the great sign of being protected, of having made it. It is something that your children can inherit, and which will ensure that they will in turn make it. The home is seen as an asset that never loses value. In turn, the rented flat is often seen as a temporary step towards homeownership – where young people live with friends before they settle down and start a family. This idea of a progression from renting to ownership and family life is a fantasy, especially as many people in cities will likely always be stuck in a private rented sector which is built on the legally enforced precariousness of tenants. But rented accommodation often has a feeling of being merely temporary, either because you will eventually be one of the lucky ones who can buy property, or because your landlord can decide to evict you at any time.

It is not surprising that many people dream of moving out of rented accommodation, and having a home of their own. The unaffordability of private renting in itself places very severe limitations on our choices. Private renters have little control over their situations – where they live, with whom, and under what conditions. Only very privileged renters can afford to live under conditions which they have chosen, while the rest have to pick between more or less undesirable options according to what they can pay for. For many, this means living with strangers in overcrowded flats. The pandemic also led to increased tensions among renters in shared properties, who often have little say over who they live with. The dream of having a home of one's own, where you won't be evicted and no one can disturb you, is in many ways a rational response to the conditions under which we live. Yet homeownership for all is not the solution to any of the problems outlined above. Not one of the many contradictions that constitute working-class life can be solved by finding 'affordable' models of private property. We delude ourselves if we believe that we can remove ourselves from the symptoms of the contradiction inherent in the housing system by participating in that very system.

This much is obvious to many on the left. But, as I noted in the introduction, we also need to make clear that simply returning to the model of council housing which dominated the twentieth century is also not an adequate option for the housing movement. While some Labour councils and more radical architects in the post-war era wanted to create more communal forms of life, none of them fundamentally challenged the private household. And while the more affordable rent of council housing made renting a more attractive option for many, the aim was a 'fairer' rent rather than the abolition of rent extraction. The homes provided by the state during the course of the twentieth century were in many cases small, poorly built, and reliant on normative assumptions about the arrangement of domestic labour and the nuclear family. And while the local council might be a better landlord than your average buy-to-let investor, there's no such thing as a good landlord. The dominant narrative of the housing crisis risks creating a nostalgic vision of post-war council housing, which overlooks the fact that the welfare state and its model of housing were an attempt to solve the problem of capitalist social reproduction – a model that continued to rely on very restrictive notions of what a home should look like and what labour should take place within it. It's easy to create dichotomies of bad private landlords versus good council homes, but there has never been a model of housing under capitalism that has actually served the needs of all parts of the proletariat.

All of this should make us think beyond the merely defensive model of housing activism that is focused on resolving the current crisis and returning to normal. Of course, in the current moment of frequent evictions and rent rises, we need to resist. Preventing and resisting evictions – defending renters' ability to stay in their homes even after they have received an eviction notice – will be a key way of protecting the lives of working-class people and building power in the coming years. Similarly, rent controls could limit the profitability of being a landlord, making it a less attractive form of exploitation. Housing discrimination against people of colour, migrants, queer people, disabled people, and benefit claimants needs to be resisted. The UK government's 'hostile environment' policies, which forces landlords to act as border guards, must be abolished. All these things are urgent, and mean that the housing movement often has its hands full. But in order to truly resist the current state of things, we also need to rethink what a home could be. This means going beyond both homeownership and the twentieth-century model of public housing as solutions to the current housing crisis – models which have always presumed not only the commodification of housing but normative family models and privatised reproductive labour.

In their very design, most of our current homes are built for nuclear families, with two, three, or four bedrooms. In Britain, many people live in one-family houses with their own garden, and often even those who don't have access to this form of housing aspire to it. Each house or flat has its own kitchen, presuming that reproductive labour such as cooking will only happen in private. The current arrangement of the domestic sphere is naturalised – it appears to be depoliticised, dehistoricised, and inherently good. The very notion of bourgeois domesticity, and the bourgeois idea of a good life, depends on a separation of the private sphere from the public. The household must therefore appear to be something separate from the society around it. This hides the labour and the violence that takes place within the home. It is often assumed, even on the left, that the private family home is what 'everyone' aspires to. When there is conflict within house shares or housing cooperatives, that is often taken as a sign that more communal forms of living are not possible, and that communal domestic arrangements inherently lead to more conflict than the private nuclear family. But when the private nuclear family home is a site of violence, that is taken to be an aberration from an otherwise healthy and desirable arrangement of our domestic lives.

It's important that in our struggle against evictions and protections against the worst aspects of the private rented sector, we don't glamourise the ideal of a secure, private home. The challenge for the housing movement lies in the question of how to do housing activism without glorifying the notion of home, how to struggle both for and against the idea of a stable and secure home as the key to our flourishing. While we build our power to protect ourselves from landlords, we need to remember that the home itself is not an unproblematic place which should simply be defended. The domestic sphere as we know it is insufficient, sometimes actively harmful. While organising to protect each other from evictions, high rents, and disrepair, we also need to dream of a better life for all of us, where home is not a delineated site marked by violence and exploitation. The idea of home as a private space needs to be challenged in everything we do.

In our struggle to build a movement around housing, we should aim to foster spaces where we can think collectively about what housing could be, beyond the confines of capitalist models of domesticity. This would be the development of a deeper engagement with housing politics – not only a struggle over the number of homes built and how much they cost to buy or rent, but an exploration of the design of homes and what kind of household structure they presume. The material structures of housing, in terms of its design and modes of ownership, both shape and are shaped by normative models of family and reproductive labour. The housing movement could be a space for breaking down the boundaries of the private/public distinction, expanding housing politics into a broader struggle over daily life. In politicising housing, we can also challenge idealised but violent and exclusionary logics of family and property.

It's hard to know exactly what more collective ways of living will look like – in many ways we can only gesture towards it. Experiments in collective forms of living often come up against very real limitations, especially as the lack of affordable and well-designed space constrains our choices of housing. But these limitations should challenge us to overcome them, not to return to the idealised private home. Struggles around housing can imply the politicisation and collectivisation of reproductive labour, through cooking together, providing childcare, and offering emotional support. This also means challenging very intimate understandings of ourselves and our daily lives. For all those who have been excluded from the white, bourgeois vision of domesticity, and for those who have been exploited and abused within it, we need to take on this challenge. Those who are currently most vulnerable to evictions and landlord harassment are also those who were never included in the pre-crisis vision of domesticity. There can be no return to normal.

2

Housing Is a Feminist Issue

In bourgeois culture, there is a myth that the home is a haven, separated from public space and the economic world of work and commerce. This ideology was strongest in the Victorian era and was then revitalised in the mid-twentieth century. Although it has long been challenged by the reality of women's participation in waged work, and by the feminist movement, the separation of home from formal workplace has been cemented into our built environment – it is ideology made into brick and concrete. And in this physically separate sphere of the home, people are expected to carry out most of the work needed to survive under capitalism. Food is prepared, children are cared for, and adults receive much of the emotional sustenance they need to carry on working. The sick, the disabled, and the elderly often prefer to receive care at home – an understandable preference given the often abysmal state of both public and private residential care facilities.

Of course, the ideological separation of the domestic and the public spheres has never been complete. Many people do receive care outside of their homes, and the nuclear household model has never been able to fully sustain itself without support from the state or paying for caring services. Nonetheless, this separation is not total fiction. For many women, the home is not a space of leisure but a place of work. Contrary to the hopes of some in the feminist movement, caregiving responsibilities have not stopped falling at the feet of women as a consequence of women entering the paid workforce en masse. As Dolores Hayden points out, women caregivers often have to orient their paid work around their caring responsibilities, so that they have the temporal and spatial flexibility to be able to pick children up from school or provide assistance for an elderly parent. This sometimes means forgoing higher-paid employment and opting for part-time work near one's home.[1]

The New York Wages for Housework Committee, a feminist group active in the 1970s, were aware of how housing struggles intersect with the struggle against the conditions of women's unwaged work in the home. In their pamphlet *A Woman's Home Is Not Her Castle*, they draw a connection between poor housing conditions and women having to work more to make this domestic space habitable. They write:

> A run-down apartment is more work for us, cleaning and scrubbing to compensate for the lack of comfort and facing all the daily crises that always fall on our shoulders. Ours is the daily battle with the roaches, the garbage that is piling up, the ceilings that are collapsing, the lack of heat

> and the long flights of stairs we have to climb with the groceries and the laundry bags. Not to mention the fights with the landlord to get things repaired that are enough to drive us crazy.[2]

While these struggles are by no means exclusive to women, the burden of attempting to make a poor-quality building into a home still often falls to wives and mothers. In my organising work in a working-class area of London, many of the people who get involved are mothers who are desperate to protect their children from the hazards of damp, mould, and other poor housing conditions. Women are responsible not only for providing care within the home, but for creating and maintaining the sense of home itself. Bad housing conditions create more work – more work scrubbing mould from the walls, more work trying to create a bit of niceness to compensate for water leaking from the ceiling, more supervision of children to make sure they don't hurt themselves on exposed wires. This work of making home, and of compensating for poor-quality housing, is never a completed endeavour – as the saying goes, a woman's work is never done.

But while women have historically been assigned almost exclusive responsibility for producing home, and thus turning a building into a space where life can be reproduced, they have lacked control of the very space they have produced. This is true both formally, in terms of women's ownership of property, and in a more informal sense of how domestic space is lived and used. Women are largely responsible for creating a sense of home where other people can relax and withdraw from the world outside, and manage conflicting needs within the family unit. The New York Wages for

Housework Committee write that mothers have to create space for children to play but also to ensure that the children don't disturb their father as he rests.[3] While this pattern is less pronounced now than it was in the 1970s, it lives on in contemporary uses of domestic space, where women rarely have any room of their own within the family home and lack their own privacy, but are constantly expected to be ready to meet other people's need for care.[4]

Not only in terms of space but also in terms of ownership of homes, women have often been disprivileged. All over the world, women have historically lacked the right to ownership of property, and even as such formal rights have been won, the financial means to access ownership has typically been missing. Hayden reminds us that in mid-twentieth-century US, while the ideology of suburban homeownership was at its peak, women were completely excluded from accessing mortgages.[5] More recently, it's been women's lower wages and lack of financial security that have often either excluded them from mortgage eligibility completely or only made them eligible for more expensive sub-prime mortgages. Single women and lone mothers were among the groups worst affected by the foreclosures following the 2008 global financial crisis, and, as usual, it was black and brown women who were most at risk of losing their homes to foreclosures.[6] Even when these groups can access the supposedly more secure form of domestic control through homeownership, it is often revealed that these homes are more or less rented from the bank, and can be taken away when it is in the interests of financial capital to do so.

High house prices and rent mean that women often struggle to access suitable housing. Women's lower wages means that there is currently no region in England where an average-priced one-bedroom would be considered affordable to a single woman on an average wage, whereas a single man on an average wage could afford an average-priced one-bedroom home anywhere in England except London.[7] The picture is similarly bleak in the US, where one in five women renters reported they were behind on rent payments in 2021, and 46.5 per cent of women renters said they were likely to face eviction within the next two months.[8] Women's labour power is seen as worth less, partly because there is an assumption that they have caring responsibilities that take away from their capacity to work full time. Thus, women are paid less because they have (or are assumed to have) a responsibility for unwaged reproductive labour. Assumptions about the family wage – which meant that men were paid more because they were supporting a family, while women were assumed to be supported by a man – remain even though that household model hasn't been dominant for a long time. People, and women especially, are often pressured into being part of a cohabiting couple, because the rent of even a single room in a shared flat is increasingly unaffordable in large cities.

For single parents, it's even harder to secure suitable homes. Having to rely on one wage and a paltry benefits system, while needing more space for their children, single parents struggle with high housing costs and are often made homeless. Because women have been made socially responsible for reproduction, about 80 per cent of single parents in the US are mothers, a figure that is even higher, at 84 per cent, in the UK.[9] This is part of the powerful incentive to raise children within a nuclear family form, even as there is less explicit social pressure to conform to traditional family norms. As Michèle Barrett and Mary McIntosh argue, single parents are both materially and ideologically disprivileged in terms of bringing up their children.[10] This means that it's not only social stigma that can account for the longevity of the heteronormative two-parent form, but also the sheer impracticality and unaffordability of raising children on one's own, especially on a woman's wage. Susanne Soederberg points to the interaction between productive and reproductive economies to understand the gendered aspects of housing, and housing as a sphere of reproduction more broadly, writing that 'single-parent households typically headed by women had to deal with the quadruple burden consisting of childcare costs, unwaged work, insufficient working hours (many working poor mothers are involuntary part-time workers) and unequal wages'. She adds,

> The forced removal of a single mother and her children from her rental home (place of survival) begins not with an eviction order initiated by her landlord and imposed by the state, but with her inability to make regular rental payments due to insufficient income. As with most tenants affected by, or living on the brink of, eviction notices, our single parent earns her money as a low-wage, low-skill worker in the service sector engaged in activities such as cleaning, property maintenance, caregiving, retail, hospitality, transportation and so forth.[11]

This means that women, despite having been granted equal legal standing to men, are often economically dependent on them, especially if they are mothers. Those who do leave a heterosexual relationship, or were never part of one in the first place, often struggle to support themselves and any children they have – facing an ever greater risk of rent arrears, debt, illness related to poor housing conditions, overcrowding, and eviction. Single mothers are vastly over-represented in temporary accommodation for homeless households. While the traditional notion of a homeless person is a single man, figures from 2018 showed that in England 67 per cent of people recognised as homeless by a local authority were women, and 66 per cent of homeless families were headed by a single mother.[12] In the US, 60 per cent of homeless households with children were headed by a woman.[13]

Women's homelessness is not caused by individual shortcomings but by structural forces related to gendered household arrangements. Paul Watt, in his study of single mothers living in temporary accommodation, found that most of the women he spoke to had been made homeless because of either family disputes (often caused or exacerbated by severe overcrowding), domestic violence, or eviction (typically due to rent arrears).[14] This echoes Soederberg's description of homelessness not as a one-off event but as part of a cycle of low-waged work, debt, arrears, and displacement.[15] To that we can add the pressures and conflicts of living in a home that is overcrowded or violent.

Domestic Violence Is a Housing Problem

The processes of caring work, low pay, and domestic abuse are all intertwined. Women's caring responsibilities and low income sometimes force them to move in with parents or other family members, or to stay in abusive relationships. Domestic violence is deeply connected to women's role within the home as caregivers and workers who lack control over the space they inhabit and work in. Women often face violence in a continuum with the social expectation that they provide a certain level of domestic comfort, and this violence thus serves as a tool of disciplining their domestic labour. If they try to leave, the violence can get worse, as it functions to keep the family unit intact. Women's lack of privacy within the home also means they often can't withdraw when interactions with partners become hostile. And the fact that the sanctity of the family home is so deeply entrenched in bourgeois culture means that the domestic space is shielded from neighbours and friends who could otherwise intervene in situations of domestic abuse. The domestic sphere can be incredibly dangerous for those who do not necessarily benefit from living in a space that has been separated from the public sphere. For many women, children, and queer and trans people (especially queer and trans youth), home is far from the safe haven it is often portrayed as. It can be a space of abuse, domination, and control. Domestic abuse is thus a housing issue not only in the sense of being a leading cause of women's homelessness, but also because the design of private homes creates shelter for harmful behaviour. The very thing that is supposed to protect people from violence – the private domestic space – becomes a source of violence and a condition for its continuation. As M. E. O'Brien puts it, 'there is a clear division in many families between behavior presented to the outside world and what is acceptable behind closed doors, creating conditions for otherwise socially unacceptable violence'.[16] Heterosexual culture is often demeaning and harmful both for queer people and for heterosexual women, who bear the brunt of the violence perpetrated in the name of love.

Violence and harassment against women is not only perpetrated by partners and ex-partners. I have heard women tenants report feeling unsafe in their homes due to sexist harassment and violence from landlords and letting agents. Such harassment often means that the tenant is no longer able to feel at home, as the constant worry about the landlord turning up without notice means that the house does not offer protection from the outside world. This is especially common for racialised women and single mothers, who face constant discrimination, harassment, and violence within a housing system largely controlled by white men. While landlord harassment can affect any renter, we should not ignore the gendered and racialised elements of landlord–tenant interactions.

The home, then, is often not a space of refuge. But leaving an abusive home is often incredibly hard, both because of emotional links that tie victims of abuse to the family and the home (which may feel like the only emotional attachments possible) and because leaving an abusive home might mean facing homelessness. Home is what we depend on, even if it is also a place of harm. If there is anything I've learnt from years of involvement in struggles around domestic violence and housing, it is that domestic violence is a housing problem. Survivors of abuse often don't want to see their partner or ex-partner in prison. Instead, their highest priority is accessing safe and stable housing. The lack of affordable and easily accessible places to live means that too many people end up staying in homes where they face violence or abuse. And those who do manage to leave suffer from the stressful and retraumatising experience of trying to access housing support from underfunded services. Not having the financial means to pay a deposit and the first month of rent, or not having a guarantor to co-sign a tenancy agreement, can also be a barrier to securing housing.[17] Tenants are typically expected to provide references from an employer and their most recent landlord, something that people suddenly having to flee violence often lack.

While most people experiencing domestic abuse are legally entitled to be rehoused by the state in the UK, in reality this support is often very difficult to access. Local councils, which are responsible for rehousing those who experience domestic violence, tend to engage in gatekeeping practices, with the result that people fleeing their homes are often unlawfully denied a safe home. This includes practices of demanding large amounts of evidence that the person seeking support is experiencing violence, long wait times to access housing, and disbelief that the survivor is actually experiencing domestic violence, to the point where survivors of abuse report regretting fleeing their homes.[18] When local councils do accept that they have an obligation to rehouse, they often place survivors in unsuitable housing in poor condition, thus exacerbating the trauma of domestic violence and homelessness. As Ellen Malos and Gill Hague point out, the loss of home can be especially traumatic for those who have worked hard to create a home under difficult circumstances. Fleeing domestic violence can mean not only the loss of relationships and support systems, but also the loss of sense of self that has become entangled with the domestic space one has worked to make and maintain.[19]

In an increasingly overburdened system of temporary accommodation provided by local authorities, women who become homeless are often displaced not only from their homes but also from the area where they used to live. It is common practice, especially in large English cities, to move homeless households to cheaper areas – sometimes in a completely different part of the country. Homeless households are forced to take whatever they are offered, as they will otherwise risk losing their right to be housed at all.

This system is often especially devastating for women. People who have experienced domestic violence are often forced to relocate to a place where they can't be easily found. Some women experiencing domestic abuse choose to stay with an abusive partner rather than being forced to leave the area they live in, so that even the threat of displacement puts women more at risk of continued violence and abuse.[20] Single mothers who are forced out of their homes by overcrowding or eviction also leave support systems behind. Especially when they are forced to move far away, they no longer have access to the informal childcare provided by friends or relatives that enabled them to have any form of life outside their home and caring responsibility. Working-class women in particular tend to depend on very site-specific forms of caring networks, such as the informal practices of shared responsibility for childcare that mothers on working-class estates often develop.[21] Placing young children in daycare centres can be incredibly expensive, way beyond the means of women who may have lost even their precarious and low-paid work in the process of becoming homeless and having to relocate. This leads women to a situation of sole responsibility for the care of young children, stuck in an unfamiliar place far from their support systems. The isolation many experience within the family home can become even worse when they are forced to leave it. Watt writes that many of his interviewees spoke of this deep sense of isolation when they were displaced through the homelessness system.[22] It's important to point out that this isolation causes not only emotional distress but more work, as the pressures of childcare increase and mothers have to try to compensate for the distress their children experience when they are made homeless.

The nexus of caring responsibilities, lack of affordable homes and decent incomes, and violence experienced by many women leads us back to a critique of the notion of home as a space sheltered from the danger and stress of the outside world. Home is not necessarily a place of rest – it is usually the space where some people have to work very hard to keep themselves and other people reasonably healthy and happy. The privacy that defenders of the bourgeois home praise can in fact be experienced as a deep isolation, which exacerbates domestic exploitation and abuse. Against romantic defences of the home, we can create a liberatory politics of home that seeks to preserve it as a space of autonomy from bosses and landlords while simultaneously questioning our domestic isolation from neighbours, friends, and members of our various communities.

Women have often been central in struggles for a different housing system. The 1915 Glasgow rent strike was famously led by proletarian women who were fed up with handing over an increasing portion of a meagre wage to their landlords. In a quieter way, women did the work that enabled the Bengali squatters' movement in 1970s East London, reproducing not only their families but the movement itself. Shabna Begum points to women's role in creating collective spaces in which the squatters could meet, eat, and socialise as an essential aspect of creating a successful movement in a hostile city.[23] These are not isolated instances, but examples of the core role that women have played in building and sustaining housing movements. As they are the very people disproportionately affected by the housing crisis, it should come as no surprise that women are at the forefront of struggles to transform the housing system as a whole.

3

Never at Home

As ideals of homeownership have once more become increasingly entrenched since the 1970s, renting has become increasingly insecure. Rents in cities across the world have gone up, forcing many people from their homes and communities. Landlords' ability to evict has in many cases been strengthened. This means that renters are often experiencing high levels of displacement, which further reinforces the idea that homeownership is the means to a secure life.

In the UK, the no-fault eviction process, also known as Section 21, has been part of the reality of private renters since it was created through the Housing Act 1988. Section 21 allows landlords to evict tenants without giving a reason. It is a tool to produce fear and compliance. It is also a tool to produce ever-increasing profits, as tenants are more likely to accept rent increases under the threat of eviction. Similar regimes of insecurity exist in, for example, the US, where the landlord does not have to give a reason for evicting the tenant after the end of the initial lease period. However, these policies are not inevitable – in many European countries, renters experience much higher levels of security, as they can only be evicted under particular circumstances. At the time of writing, the conservative UK government has spent five years promising to abolish Section 21, as the destabilising effect of this policy has become increasingly obvious. But due to fierce resistance from landlords and their friends within the Tory Party, Section 21 still exists, and still impacts the lives of most private renters.

The reason why rents in the UK, and particularly in London, have been rising so dramatically over the past few decades is that Section 21 allows landlords to evict tenants quickly and easily. Should renters request that their homes be maintained or that rents be kept at a lower level, landlords can just evict them, often without a court hearing. When landlords don't have to give a reason to evict, anything that threatens the profitability of owning a home that can be let becomes a legitimate cause for eviction. The fear of eviction comes to dominate the lives of those private renters who haven't even been given an eviction notice. We're too scared to do anything that might upset our landlords, including exercising our rights as tenants.

What forms of subjectivity do no-fault evictions produce? Private renters are isolated from one another and made to compete over the few available homes we can afford. When it comes to housing – a central aspect of our selves and our daily lives – we often cannot experience ourselves as actors with agency to substantially change our circumstances. At most, if things get too unbearable, we move to a different place, where things might be as bad but in a slightly different way.

By the term subjectivity, I mean not only how we understand our selves, but also what we come to expect from our lives and how we view our place in the world. If you probably have to move on in six months or a year, you're unlikely to be able to form any deep sense of belonging in your home or your local area. Peter Marcuse and David Madden describe the deep sense of precarity that current housing systems produce as a lack of 'ontological security', by which they mean 'the sense that the stability of the world can be taken for granted. It is the emotional foundation that allows us to feel at ease in our environment and at home in our housing.'[1] In legal regimes where the landlord has the right to evict without giving a reason, renters come to expect to be moved on. They therefore cannot take this emotional security for granted. Their existence in one place is always temporary. They are always at risk of not only losing their homes, but having to move far away from jobs, schools, friends, and relatives.

The Assured Shorthold Tenancy (AST) regime, of which Section 21 is a key aspect, was designed to be maximally profitable for landlords and minimally secure for renters. This insecurity and profitability are two sides of the same coin. An AST is a fixed-term contract which can be as short as six months, after which the tenancy automatically becomes a periodic tenancy – meaning the landlord can use the Section 21 process to end it at any time. This effectively undermines many of the legal rights that renters do have – if we insist that those rights are respected, the landlord might tell us to leave. The law is not only a system of legal acts, courts, and judges. Perhaps more importantly, it is the creation of forms of subjectivity that encourage people to act or not act in specific ways. Private renters, living with the spectre of Section 21, are less likely to demand their legal right to live in a home fit for human habitation, free from serious hazards or obvious structural damage. Instead, we come to accept what is offered to us, which is mostly homes in a sorry state. Some 21 per cent of homes in the private rented sector in England do not live up to the Decent Homes Standard, which requires that homes are free from serious risks to health and safety.[2]

In the legal regime created by the Housing Act 1988, you can never be fully at home in the house or flat you rent. As renters, we're always aware that our homes belong to someone else, and that they can be taken away at any time after the initial six months of the fixed-term tenancy have elapsed. For women in particular, often disproportionately responsible for the work of making a house into a home, frequent evictions carry not only the economic costs of moving vans and deposits, but also the labour of trying to turn each new dwelling into somewhere to feel at home. Evictions are disruptive of these homemaking efforts, and create a sense not only of handing over most of your money while getting little in return, but also of expending a lot of work trying to make a place feel like home, only to have to do it all over again a year later. And if we start to relate to our homes too much – replacing the furniture, putting up pictures on the wall, or keeping pets – we risk not only eviction but having our deposits taken away. So we try to change as little as possible during our temporary stay in someone else's house. This temporary stay might be six months or many years. The point is that you can never quite know how long you will be there, because it depends on the whims of landlords and their agents.

The very profitable insecurity that tenants on ASTs experience is often facilitated by letting agents. Agents are parasites upon parasites, taking a cut of the rent you pay your landlord for their often questionable 'services' while encouraging landlords to maximise profitability. Rents can increase much more quickly if there is a high turnover – when people have short tenancies and your landlord or their agent can simply turf you out and replace you with a higher-paying tenant whenever they see fit to do so. So we don't put down roots. We don't turn the places we rent into homes. We prepare to move on as soon as the fixed term of the tenancy ends, hoping to stay but ready to go. Many renters who have been told to move out do so before the end of the notice period, and before the landlord has to go to court for a possession order. Some don't know they have a legal right to stay after the notice has expired, or even that they have a right to stay after the fixed term of their tenancy has ended. Others feel like it's not worth fighting an eviction, since contesting it in court might slow down the process but is unlikely to stop it. Better to move on, and save yourself the trouble.

Section 21 means that we have to be mobile, always moving around to find somewhere we can afford. The area you live in might become unaffordable very quickly, as a result of landlords' hunger for increasing profits. Private renting is a core cause of gentrification. Renters simply get told the rent is going up, often with little notice. If they refuse the increase or try to negotiate, they will likely get served a Section 21 notice, to be replaced by someone who's willing to pay the increased rent. They may then find that all the available homes in the area have become unaffordable to them, and be pushed further out to the fringes of the city, where they replace someone even worse off.

The minimal protections against rent increases that we do have are pretty much useless for two reasons. First, people who contest a rent increase through the First-tier Tribunal system are likely to be served an eviction notice, or the worry that they will be evicted will prevent them from contesting the increase in the first place. Second, the Tribunal can only set rents at market levels, which means that those who are being pushed out of their neighbourhoods by quickly increasing rents have very little hope of success in bringing their own rent down. Only those whose landlords have set the rent at a higher level than other properties in the area have any chance of succeeding. In fact, the Tribunal can increase the rent set by the landlord, if it's judged to be below market level. No wonder very few people use this system. As Nick Bano points out, Section 21 renders any form of rent control toothless, and ensures that renters quietly accept handing over most of their income to their landlords.[3] These large sums of money that we are made to part with each month are the opposite of an investment – they do not accumulate value, or even ensure the maintenance of your home, but instead just disappear into the bottomless pockets of your landlord (and the pockets of letting agents and banks), never to be seen again.

Manufactured bidding wars and open viewings (when all prospective tenants are made to attend a viewing at the same time to show how much competition there is for a home) are tools letting agents use to tell tenants that there is more scarcity in housing than there actually is, and therefore create more acceptance of paying a much higher price for the same abysmal service. If these worrisome trends continue, they might become established as part of the culture of private renting – what tenants expect when they're looking for a new home. Landlords and agents are currently putting rents up because everyone else is doing it. This forces renters to accept handing over even more of their income to their landlord, as they would struggle to find somewhere else where they could pay less. These increases do not always reflect any increased mortgage costs for the landlords, as they often either have fixed interest rates or have already paid off the mortgage.[4] Instead, landlords and agents increase the rents because they can. They control access to something people need to live, and therefore, if they act together, they can basically set whichever price they want.

However, there are limits to people's ability to pay. Stagnant wages, unemployment, illness, increased energy prices, and the high cost of childcare mean that many renters struggle, even before they are told their rent is going up. This is where easy evictions are very handy for landlords. Section 21 is a leading cause of homelessness in England.[5] Most people who get served a Section 21 notice have their home taken from them, but they manage to find a new one. But with higher costs of living, the rate of inflation and wage stagnation, increased rents, and high pressure on the rental market, lots of people who would normally be able to avoid homelessness following an eviction notice are now more at risk of having to sleep on sofas or on the streets. This fear of homelessness – the risk that things might not work out if you get evicted – impacts renter consciousness, especially when things are bad. Many renters don't have savings or a significant safety net. Many of us would struggle to raise a new deposit before our current deposit is returned (if it is returned). As one renter points out, looking for a new home can become like a part-time job, and even if we spend hours every day looking for a new home, there are no guarantees we will find somewhere to move.[6] While Section 21 means that we have to be mobile, many renters just aren't. They get stuck in a place between tenancies, sometimes after a judge has given the landlord a possession order and there is a warrant for bailiffs to evict them. Local authorities are legally obligated to support people at risk of homelessness. But as they don't have the financial means to do this for everyone who needs it, council homelessness teams often develop a culture of gatekeeping, deliberately misinforming renters about their rights and demanding people jump through hoops to access even minimal support. Here, we need to consider not only the health impact of homelessness itself, but also the mental health impact of the threat of homelessness and widespread housing precarity. Wondering whether one will have somewhere to live tomorrow or in a year's time can easily become an all-consuming thought. The local state, which is supposed to help people facing homelessness, often directly contributes to this emotional damage by applying policies in a punitive and arbitrary fashion.

Many people seek an individualised exit from the insecurity of the private rented sector, through homeownership. But the security of some people is founded on the insecurity of others. Madden and Marcuse refer to the opposite of ontological security as residential alienation. This is a state of never feeling at home.[7] But instead of thinking of residential alienation as something that can be overcome through bourgeois, privatised notions of domesticity, we should consider it as an inevitable outcome of a housing system that privileges the financial and domestic security of homeowners over that of renters.

As house prices have continued to increase for decades (with just a short period of slowdown after the 2008 financial crisis) buying one's home becomes increasingly unrealistic for a vast population of renters. Those on the lowest incomes will never be able to access mortgages to buy their own home. Instead renters come to expect a lifetime of moving between increasingly expensive but low-quality homes, which eat up a very high proportion of their income. In London, the average rent of a one-bedroom flat is half of the average monthly wage.[8] Low-income renters are even worse off. Even with housing benefits, those on the lowest incomes will often pay the biggest proportion of their income to landlords, who do very little for them in return. Making social renting unattainable for most people and private renting incredibly insecure can act as a way to shore up aspirations for homeownership. But if renting becomes too insecure and expensive for renters, they become trapped in a situation where they can't save up money for a deposit to buy, thus undermining the material possibilities of buying oneself out of the private rented sector. Renters can therefore become stuck in a state of desiring the security homeownership seems to promise, but with no way of actually attaining it, and instead having to accept insecurity and sky-high rents.

Instead of moving out as soon as we get served an eviction notice, or even when the fixed term of our tenancy has ended, what would happen if we insisted on staying put when the landlord told us to leave? First and foremost, it would increase the cost to the landlord, and therefore decrease the profitability of landlordism. This challenge to landlord profits depends not only on renters winning more legal rights, but on a cultural and subjective shift. We need to learn that we can and should ask for more, so that landlords will have less. A central role of the housing movement is to foster a culture in which more people are willing to become troublesome renters, who will not peacefully move on but instead drag the eviction process out for as long as possible. This can even include a refusal to leave when bailiffs come knocking. In my work as a housing organiser, I regularly participate in eviction resistances – when a group of people come together to put their bodies in the way of bailiffs trying to reclaim possession on behalf of the landlord. Through these direct actions, we can delay evictions even after the legal process has run its course, which serves the double purpose of both giving the renter more time to find a new home and annoying the landlord. These are also important displays of solidarity and collective power, as we can shift our individualised subjectivity of fear of evictions into a collective subjectivity where we have the power to say if an eviction can take place or not. Tenants' unions across the world use eviction resistance as a core tool for building and strengthening our organisations, and they are powerful because they work on different levels at the same time. Eviction resistances are deeply practical, in that they serve to keep a roof over someone's head, but they are simultaneously symbolic, in that they challenge the very power imbalance between renters and landlords, and the isolation and fragmentation of renters as a group.

This isolation is not a natural fact, but is due to decades of political prioritisation of landlords' right to profit over renters' right to homes. Up until now, successive Tory and Labour governments have remained committed to the AST regime. This can be traced to the neoliberal state's market-enabling role. Instead of building public housing, the Thatcher government decided to focus on building a private market for rental homes. When creating ASTs and Section 21, the Tories in one fell swoop recreated the private rented sector, which had led an increasingly marginalised existence since the creation of a public rented sector in the early twentieth century. As Marxist theorists such as Ruth Wilson Gilmore have long argued, the state under neoliberalism has not so much shrunk as shifted its capacities. Gilmore calls this the anti-state state – a state that claims to be against its own existence but has in fact expanded its punitive capacities and invested its resources in enabling market-provided 'solutions' to replace the welfare state.[9] UK governments' commitment to expanding the increasingly unaffordable private rented sector instead of investing in public housing costs billions of pounds in public money every year – money that the government hands directly to private landlords in the form of housing benefits.[10] The neoliberal state, in both its Tory and Labour guises, has thus shifted its investment from the supply side (building and investing in public housing) to the demand side (creating ever-increasing effective demand for private renting by subsidising private rents through housing benefits). The neoliberal state, it seems, disagrees with the old saying that all landlords are bastards. Instead, it suggests that all landlords are good landlords apart from the state itself.

Goodbye to No-Fault Evictions

The issues with Section 21 have been widely acknowledged for years. It seems that parts the state might finally be willing to admit that there are at least some bad landlords out there, though of course they are just a few rotten apples. In 2019, following many years of campaigning by dedicated housing activists, Theresa May's Tory Party put a promise to end Section 21 in its manifesto, in a bid to win over some renters to its otherwise homeowner-dominated voter base. Over the following years, the Renters Reform Bill slowly emerged to fulfil that promise.

At the time of writing, the Renters Reform Bill has not yet become law. But even when it does, evictions will still be a regular occurrence. More letting agents and landlords will likely start to give people licence agreements rather than tenancies to avoid the new legislation, giving renters even less protection against eviction and disrepair. But the requirement for landlords to give some kind of reason for wanting their tenants to move out puts more pressure on them to show that they are actually following the right procedures, rather than having an absolute right to evict. This serves to shift the burden of providing evidence from tenant to landlord, even if they won't have to produce much evidence. Hopefully this will lead to more tenants using their right to defend themselves in court, and thus frustrate landlords' hopes for a smooth eviction process.

Landlords worry that, without Section 21, it will become more difficult to turf out people in rent arrears and 'problem' tenants (including tenants who ask that their legal rights are respected). As soon as there is even a hint of pro-renter legislation, private landlords tend to start threatening to sell up and leave the market. They seem to assume that everyone shares their own high estimation of the services they provide, and that the idea that landlords may stop being landlords is a worrying prospect. But instead we may just shrug and say good riddance. The abolition of Section 21 will be a good opportunity to question the whole existence of the private rented sector. If even a semblance of effective rights for tenants means that landlords are no longer making enough money to feel it's worth their while, there is no reason why we couldn't expand the public rented sector instead. As I argue elsewhere in this book, a nostalgic return to post-war council housing should not be the end goal of the housing movement. We need a new system of collectively owned and managed housing, which would also entail a broader deprivatisation of the domestic sphere and closer integration of the home and collective forms of care. But if used well, this political moment could seriously weaken profit-making in homes. We can turn this into a crisis for the current housing system as a whole. This could in turn open up new possibilities for something new and better.

Landlords, the bourgeoisie, and their ideological outlets such as the *Telegraph* had a fairly panicked reaction to the abolition of the AST regime – a regime that serves to shore up housing prices, and therefore the UK economy more broadly.[11] We don't yet know exactly how the new law will work out in practice if ASTs are at last phased out in the coming years. But even before the Renters Reform Bill has become law, I have seen it empower renters to make demands on letting agents and landlords. It has shifted expectations of what we can demand, and with it, it has opened up greater possibilities for organising. Suddenly renters feel more confident to challenge benefits discrimination and demand to keep pets. This new-found confidence is a result of the end of the AST regime itself, which created a massive and insecure private rented sector but also created a population of increasingly fed-up renters. We have fought for these changes. The gains are important, because they can enable renters to feel more powerful. The cultural and subjective shift that becomes possible is as important as our increased legal rights. Anything that can shift the balance of power even a little bit might make a big difference. What could seem like a banal legal reform could become an opportunity to organise more renters, and to enable more of us to say that we won't accept walls covered with mould, dodgy electrics, and rent increases at many times the rate of inflation.

The law won't save us. Only a strong and confident renters' movement will be able to force the changes we need – a system in which renters are empowered to demand their rights and more. We need to practise exercising our rights. The more we all do this, the harder it will become for landlords to kick us out in order to replace us with more compliant tenants. We need to learn about our rights as well as their limitations, and where we have enough leverage to challenge landlords' and agents' hunger for profits. As Bano writes, the housing movement has long been busy 'pouring sand into the gearbox of the housing-wealth-generation machine'.[12] This can create a subjective shift in which we go from an emotional state characterised by isolation and fear of our landlords to one dominated by collective anger at a system that exploits us. The coming years will be a time of intense struggle over the content and practice of the new law. In the meantime, let's keep building our power, learning our rights, resisting evictions, and demanding more for renters.

4

Poor Housing Creates Poor Health

As someone who moved to the UK as an adult, I found it hard to adjust to worse housing conditions than I was used to. It was mainly the poor insulation of homes that was striking – homes get very cold in the winter, despite outdoor temperatures being warmer than in my home country. I had to learn to wear several layers of clothing inside during winter. As the cost-of-living crisis has made clear, we spend a lot of money heating up energy-inefficient homes, which allow heat to leak through windows, door frames, walls, and roofs. Not only is this bad for our health, causing thousands of deaths each year,[1] but it also means that our consumption of energy is much greater than it could be. Insulating homes properly would be one of the easiest ways of reducing energy consumption in order to stave off climate disaster. It seems to make sense to invest a lot of resources in properly insulating the housing stock, but progress has been painfully slow.

The related issues of damp and mould were also things that struck me when I first moved to the UK. In my twenties, all the houses I lived in had problems with mould, and while I can't remember seeing black mould in anyone's house before I moved here, I quickly had to get used to it. Mould is indeed quite normalised – it's just one of the things you have to live with if you're a renter. Both private and social landlords have a tendency to blame the problem on tenants. It's supposedly because we conduct activities such as cooking, bathing, washing and drying clothes – even breathing excessively – that mould appears. But people in other countries also perform these activities, which might in fact be a normal part of what it means to live somewhere. And yet those same activities do not produce walls completely black with mould in countries with a better housing stock, so it would seem that issues with damp and mould are related to the sorry state of housing in the UK. This was what the report 'Spotlight on damp and mould: It's not lifestyle' concluded, urging landlords to stop blaming tenants for mould growth.[2] If mould is a result of condensation, landlords should take action to better ventilate our homes. Moreover, mould often appears as a result not of condensation but of persistent damp in the walls, or even leaking pipes that aren't fixed. But even when there is an obvious leak causing damage to the property and producing health hazards in the form of mould, landlords are often slow to react because tenants' health is not a priority for them.

It's a well-known fact that many people today are living in homes that are damaging their health. Health issues related to poor housing conditions cost the NHS around £1.4 billion every year.[3] In the US, a privatised healthcare system means that renters not only have to live with poor housing conditions but also have to take responsibility for the resulting medical costs. Newspaper headlines and TV documentaries regularly reveal the squalor in which working-class people live. These accounts tend to produce moments of public anger, as we bear witness to the dangerous conditions that landlords make people live in.

And yet there has been little action taken to resolve the problems that lead to poor conditions in the first place – perhaps because doing so would challenge the very foundations on which the contemporary housing system has been built. Poor conditions in council and housing association homes are often the direct result of decades of underfunding for the maintenance of ageing and often poorly built housing stock. And in the private rented sector, the fact that landlords can get away with spending very little money on repairs and maintenance means that they are able to make more profit. This, in turn, shores up the national economy more widely by preventing the housing market from collapsing. Reforms to compel private landlords to improve standards have not been in line with government aims to maintain house prices at all cost.[4] Because the national economies of the UK and other countries in Europe and North America are anchored to property prices, and private landlords own a significant part of the housing stock, anything that would threaten the profitability of landlordism could also have significant consequences for the economy as a whole. However, even the Tory government has begun to acknowledge that we do need to challenge the abhorrent state of disrepair and poor conditions that plague the UK housing stock, across the private rented, social, and owner-occupied sectors.

Most housing issues, such as dangerous electrics and gas appliances, broken or faulty windows, leaking pipes, missing safety features, collapsing ceilings, and flooding, fall within landlords' legal responsibilities. But landlords are often painfully slow to act. As we have seen, private renters are scared to complain too much, given that they can easily be evicted, but even when they do complain, landlords have few incentives to carry out structural repairs. Instead, they are more inclined to 'fix' issues with mould and damp by applying a layer of paint or at most a bit of plaster. Tenants in social housing have to deal with overstretched and bureaucratic repairs procedures and outsourced maintenance companies, sometimes finding themselves waiting for months or years before their complaints are even acknowledged.

Capitalism creates conditions that are damaging to many people's health. Workplace accidents, stress, food poverty, and limited access to healthcare and emotional support all contribute to the damage of life under capitalism. In their book *Health Communism*, Beatrice Adler-Bolton and Artie Vierkant argue that capitalist society continually marks some people as surplus to the needs of capitalist accumulation. They draw on Marx's theorisation of surplus populations, which outlines how the people who don't have access to secure employment are an essential aspect of capitalist economies. People who are un- or underemployed serve to hold down wages, as employed workers continually have the threat of being made redundant hanging over their heads, preventing them from demanding too much of their employers. Adler-Bolton and Vierkant theorise how this surplus population is partly made up of people who are disabled or too sick to work. Drawing on Marta Russell's theorisation of disability as a condition created by capital's categorisation of some people as less productive than the 'normal' worker,[5] Adler-Bolton and Vierkant suggest that disability is one way that people get thrown out of the productive economy and come to be regarded as 'waste'. As they write, 'Waste – surplus populations – are policed and certified by capitalist states to demarcate the boundary of who is an acceptable member of the body politic, with all who fall outside of this normative frame labelled as a burden.'[6] Capitalism always needs to turn some people into surplus.

This understanding of the surplus population is instructive for thinking about housing conditions, because the capitalist state has since its inception been concerned with how workers live and die. Housing has had a central role here – as housing is the container of much reproductive labour and daily life activities, it can act as a key cause of health or illness. While individual capitalists have little interest in what their workers do once they leave the workplace, capitalist society as a whole has a vested interest in maintaining a minimal standard of working-class reproduction, lest too many people start to die or become disabled in a way that disrupts the circuit of capitalist accumulation. This is thus not a benevolent form of care for the poor (although bourgeois philanthropists may perceive their own activity as such) but a way of capitalism ensuring there are enough people who are able to work, *and* enough people who are marked as surplus.

The people who are regarded as superfluous to the capitalist workforce are typically abandoned in squalid housing conditions, because whether they live or die is of little concern to the capitalist class. There will always be more people who can be branded as surplus, and their health has no productive function to the capitalist economy. While slum clearance became a priority for the capitalist class in the nineteenth century, as it became clear that hazardous living conditions were impacting the health and therefore the productivity of the working class, many people were left in the slums. As Daniel Renwick and Robbie Shilliam have argued, some people were in fact seen as part of the slums – the fact that they had been branded as outside of the category of the 'deserving' poor meant that their places of habitation themselves came to be regarded as slums, regardless of the conditions of their homes. Renwick and Shilliam point out that this separation of the deserving and undeserving poor mapped onto a process of racialisation, in which the undeserving surplus came to be regarded as a 'caste apart'.[7]

This process continued throughout the twentieth century, as white workers' housing conditions were improved but black and brown people were often kept in squalid conditions, due to discriminatory rules around access to council housing as well as many private landlords' racism. Slum clearances displaced the poorest and most precarious people, forcing them to move into equally bad housing somewhere else. Over the past decades, this association of race and poor housing conditions has intensified through a moralising discourse on 'sink estates', which states that the moral conduct of residents is simultaneously the cause and the consequence of the decline of the housing stock.[8] Renwick and Shilliam argue that while housing conditions for everyone have been increasingly privatised – construed as an individual's responsibility to satisfy through the market – those who have been marked as surplus are increasingly criminalised, and therefore not seen as deserving of decent housing.[9] This push to criminalise includes racialised populations who have remained on dilapidated urban estates, those who have been pushed to the margins of cities and are surviving in squalid private rented housing, 'benefit scroungers', and 'illegal' migrants who must be prevented from skipping the queue for housing.

Renwick and Shilliam also point to a gendered aspect of these criminalising discourses, as residents of stigmatised estates are regularly disparaged as 'problem families' – people who are not reproducing themselves according to white, normatively gendered family patterns.[10] In this light, slum clearances emerge as an attack on proletarian forms of social reproduction that don't conform to bourgeois norms, and therefore need to be reconstituted elsewhere. In this, the slum clearances of the twentieth century are similar to estate demolition today, which not only seeks to repurpose urban land for more profitable use but also breaks apart the networks of criminalised ways of life that characterise the 'sink estate'.

Black, brown, and migrant people are more likely to live in hazardous housing conditions, and are also more likely to live in areas with dangerous levels of air pollution.[11] But it is not only members of the surplus population who live in squalid conditions. Increasingly, working-class people in regular employment, and renters more broadly, are affected by poor housing. Housing is making many people sick, but not everyone is affected by this illness to the same degree. The people who have been marked as disposable – either those who are not working or those in low-waged, precarious, and unskilled work – are disproportionately affected. This is especially the case for migrants – the people the welfare state has always been most unwilling to accept responsibility for. Seasonal migrant workers, who come to work for a few months before they are made to go back to their countries of origin, are forced to live in expensive and dangerous caravans while harvesting fruit and vegetables.[12] These people are employed, but also disposable – the state hasn't paid anything for their education or healthcare, and, should they be harmed by their housing conditions, they can always be replaced by new migrants the following year.

Race and disability or chronic illness can be thought together through a framework of social reproduction and the production of excluded and criminalised surplus populations. In fact, the social category of race is one which *produces* disability, as exposure to the worst conditions of capitalist societies leads to the worst health outcomes. Often relegated to substandard housing, racialised groups have to live with conditions that produce what Lauren Berlant calls 'slow death'.[13] Being marked as surplus means that the state is not overly concerned if the housing conditions you live in produce asthma, depression, or disability. The role of the state, then, is to ensure that the 'deserving' workers have what they need to be able to keep going to work, and that the undeserving surplus can't access the resources they would need to have a decent standard of life. The function of the surplus is also a psychological one – by ensuring that the living conditions of those seen as undeserving are below the minimum standard set by the state, the 'deserving' workers live in fear of being marked as surplus. The state, in its various guises, thus performs the labour of categorising the different sections of the working class, and gatekeeps resources from those deemed undeserving.

The conflation of housing conditions and a particular form of subjectivity – the assumption that those who live in squalid housing somehow deserve this – means that poor housing is stigmatising. In addition to the physical health effects of damp, mould, and cold, and the strain of having to try to make the best of a bad situation, there is the additional emotional damage of being implicitly or explicitly labelled as undeserving of a decent home. Renters I meet who live with disrepair and poor conditions sometimes mention feelings of shame, as if the conditions in which they live were an expression of their character. The individualising and privatising discourse around housing contributes to this, as it conveniently places the burden of securing decent housing on the individual. The tendency to blame issues such as mould on individual behaviour also serves to stigmatise individuals and obscures structural issues.

This abdication of responsibility for the housing conditions of the surplus population (and those who are continually threatened with being marked surplus) means that the state does not have to accept responsibility for poor housing conditions – instead they appear as a natural fact. It is not anyone *doing* anything that leads to poor housing conditions and worse health outcomes for the surplus; instead, it is a *non-doing* that results in slow death. Of course, this non-doing is not unintentional. Drawing on Ruth Wilson Gilmore's work, Adler-Bolton and Vierkant and Renwick and Shilliam respectively describe this as organised abandonment or organised negligence.[14] The thing about organised abandonment or negligence is that it's hard to say exactly who created the conditions for the slow (or in some cases, quick) death of residents of squalid housing. As the case of the Grenfell Tower fire showed all too clearly, legal structures are designed to shield individuals and institutions from blame.[15] Given that our legal system is set up to punish individuals, there are often calls to assign individual responsibility in the aftermath of death as a result of poor housing. But the structures of corporate law and the processes of state bureaucracy in fact reveal a truth about these deaths – there was no individual to blame; rather, the whole system is complicit. Here, it is useful to return to Friedrich Engels' phrase 'social murder': 'murder against which no one can defend himself, which does not seem what it is, because no man sees the murderer, because the death of the victim seems a natural one, since the offence is more one of omission than commission'.[16] In these supposedly natural deaths, the victims are often seen as the causes of their own suffering; if they had been deserving, the assumption goes, they would have not have lived in such dangerous environments.

As long as these conditions are limited to criminalised, racialised, and disabled surplus populations, the state tends to adopt a hands-off approach to the housing conditions of the poor. There are laws that regulate housing standards, but these are rarely enforced. Local councils, which on paper have the power and responsibility to ensure housing standards don't fall below a basic minimum, lack the financial resources to either improve their own housing stock or enforce standards in the private rented sector. Disabled and elderly people are regularly abandoned in homes that are completely unfit for their needs. The local state has been made responsible for much of the work of sorting and categorising people into deserving and undeserving, workers and surplus, and this gatekeeping regularly leads to serious harm to those who are regarded as surplus. But this harm is usually not considered much of a problem – how members of the surplus population live and die has rarely been cause for public outrage.

Engels writes that the bourgeoisie (and the capitalist state) only become interested in the housing conditions of the working class when those conditions facilitate the spread of epidemics, which then risk impacting the rich side of the town.[17] The Covid pandemic did indeed lead to increasing concern for the unsanitary and overcrowded housing conditions of poor people. But Engels, writing before the full development of bourgeois philanthropy and the eventual emergence of the welfare state, underestimated the concern the capitalist state has shown for the living conditions of the working class in times of open and generalised reproductive crisis. Stuart Hall and Bill Schwarz define crisis as a situation when 'the existing social formation can no longer be reproduced on the basis of the preexisting system of social relations'.[18] That is, the normal functioning of society can no longer carry on as it has. Crises can happen for a lot of different reasons, but crises of social reproductions happen when the normal and expected harms of life under capitalism become so widespread and severe that they threaten to disrupt the exploitation of the working class, and therefore also threaten capitalist accumulation.

This happened in the nineteenth century, before the invention of the welfare state, when members of the working class died too quickly and failed to produce healthy enough children who could become the next generation of workers.[19] The welfare state can be seen as a response to this reproductive crisis, trying to ensure productivity by establishing a baseline of reproductive support for the working class. Since the decimation of the welfare state, reproductive crises are always just about to break out, and the role of the austerity state is to do the bare minimum to ensure that reproductive crises are contained among those who can be marked as the undeserving poor. It is only when crisis conditions become too generalised, and start to affect the working class more broadly, that the state sees fit to intervene. This is why the term 'housing crisis' has gained traction in recent years – not because squalid, overcrowded, and unaffordable housing is a new or re-emerging phenomenon, but because these conditions are no longer limited to surplus populations. Berlant writes that 'when scholars and activists apprehend the phenomenon of slow death in long-term conditions of privation they choose to misrepresent the duration and scale of the situation by calling a *crisis* that which is a fact of life and has been a defining fact of life for a given population that lives it as a fact of ordinary time'.[20] But for those outside that given population, the slow death that is ordinary for the surplus population becomes unacceptable, unliveable.

When conditions of slow death are generalised, media and politicians tend to get interested in social reproduction. In recent media coverage of poor housing conditions, there has been a focus on visible disrepair, such as mould, pests, collapsing ceilings, and sewage leaks. The ITV documentary *Surviving Squalor* visually represented some truly awful living conditions, where primarily black, brown, migrant, and disabled people had been abandoned in conditions that were damaging their health. Following *Surviving Squalor*, journalists became more interested in the topic, and sought out housing conditions that were at least as bad as those represented on ITV. Housing issues that weren't easily represented visually, such as extreme temperatures or draught, were of lesser interest. Visual representations were used to turn squalor into a scandal. Images that could produce shock in the assumed middle-class or bourgeois viewer suddenly became a treasured journalistic commodity, especially when children were involved, as children are typically seen as innocent and therefore naturally deserving. There has been a tendency to redefine the residents affected by extreme housing conditions as deserving poor rather than undeserving scroungers and migrants. This work of redefinition sometimes maintains the very divisions that it seeks to challenge.

It is also striking that much of the news coverage of poor housing conditions has been centred on social housing, provided by councils and housing associations, despite the fact that conditions in the private rented sector are worse. This risks playing into a narrative that social housing is inherently poorer quality. It is true that housing associations and councils are often terrible landlords. But this is not because they are *public* landlords – it's because they are landlords. They therefore have at least a short-term interest in neglecting the needs of their tenants, and preserving their money and resources. But the government uses this negligence as an excuse to punish bad social landlords by threatening to cut their funding, thus risking making conditions worse for renters.

Perhaps the most obvious example of the dangerous housing conditions the working class are forced to live with is the Grenfell fire, in which seventy-two people lost their lives because of organised neglect by the local state. Here, death was not slow but sudden. It is also striking that 41 per cent of disabled residents of the tower block died in the fire, as few adjustments had been made that would have allowed them to escape.[21] The use of flammable building materials that contributed to residents' deaths was not something that would typically be seen as disrepair or squalor, in a visual culture where those words have been associated with dilapidation rather than shiny new cladding. But state deregulation and austerity measures had made it possible for local authorities to 'solve' issues of poor housing conditions by making 'improvements' that were in fact more dangerous than the previous conditions.[22] In such cases, social murder becomes more a form of doing than non-doing, but assigning individual blame is still difficult, as the ultimate source of the problem sits with successive governments that have been too interested in preserving the profitability of an increasingly deregulated building sector. This deregulation itself becomes a form of non-doing, of not accepting responsibility for ensuring that any 'improvements' are actually safe.

The case of Awaab Ishak, a two-year-old black child who died from mould exposure in 2020, also brings into stark relief how unaccountable the state and its outsourced service providers are. The family has spoken clearly about the racism that led to Awaab's death, as the housing association Rochdale Boroughwide Housing dismissed their appeals for help with the mould issue, and declared that the mould was caused by the family's behaviour. A manager commented that the mould was acceptable, since the family were refugees and therefore were lucky to have a roof over their heads.[23]

Hopefully the repeated tragedies of deadly housing conditions will lead to action from the government, better enforcement, stronger forms of redress for tenants, and proper investment in social housing. Indeed, if this is truly a crisis, things will have to change, as the present state of things has become untenable, and the state can no longer ensure the smooth functioning of capitalist reproduction. But when we call for change, we need to make sure we're not reproducing distinctions of deserving and undeserving, by suggesting that *these people* did not deserve to have died as they did.

In short, we should heed Adler-Bolton and Vierkant's call to centre the surplus in our political organising.[24] Migrants, disabled people, criminalised, pathologised and racialised people, those receiving benefits, and those living outside of normative forms of family or employment have been continually neglected by the capitalist state. Government intervention in their housing situations has often made things worse, rather than better. These groups also need to be able to articulate what housing conditions they need, rather than having the assumed benevolence of the state extended to them. This benevolence has always been conditional, and has always been deeply harmful to populations that do not live up to ideals of good and productive citizenship. A return to the forms of housing provision that became dominant in the mid-twentieth century won't necessarily resolve the issues with their housing conditions, as surplus populations have always been relegated to the worst part of the housing stock. These groups cannot easily be included in a more expansive conception of state-provided housing, because part of the state's job is to reproduce the structural exclusions that characterise capitalist society.

In centring the surplus, we must also maintain a critical perspective on the state, and highlight the state's role in ensuring the conditions of capitalist exploitation and accumulation. Simplistic distinctions between bad market-provided housing and good state-provided housing don't do justice to those who have always struggled to survive at the margins of the welfare state. It is only by simultaneously struggling against the state and private markets that we can begin to get closer to the housing that all of the proletariat (surplus populations included) actually need. When we call for public housing for all, we need to make sure we build a system in which those who have lived outside the boundaries of the deserving poor have their needs met and their autonomy respected. Otherwise we risk reproducing a system of paternalistic benevolence, which seeks to rehabilitate some of the surplus population into good workers and consumers, while discarding those who can't or won't be integrated into the model of the productive citizen.

5

The Feeling of Ownership

Domestic spaces are becoming increasingly haunted by the spectre of intruders and crime. There are more and more attempts to design away the prospect of unwanted people entering the private sphere. These projects are meant to foster a feeling of control over domestic space – a sense that you can and should exercise extensive surveillance of your home and its surroundings in order to protect yourself and your family from external dangers. In this way, the private household is becoming increasingly isolated, and increasingly important for meeting its members' need for security. Its ideal domestic space, the detached one-family home, is designed to create a sense of seclusion. In this way, we can understand homeownership not just as a legal and economic framework, but also as a feeling of control – of being able to exclude strangers.

The UK-based police programme Secured by Design, first launched in 1989, produces extensive design guidelines for how to integrate crime prevention into the built environment. It also gives out awards for housing developments that embody crime prevention, and its website boasts that 'police forces throughout the UK have specially trained Designing Out Crime Officers'.[1] The increased use of design features such as homelessness spikes, preventing homeless people from sleeping on benches and in more sheltered areas, is the effect of a way of thinking that seeks to design away social issues, and make sure that people can't meet any of their needs outside of the private sphere of the home. Cara Chellew has referred to this tendency to remove things we need from the public sphere as 'ghost amenities' – the traces of a different ideal of public life.[2] Meanwhile, in the domestic sphere, Sophie K. Rosa notes that 'the uncomradely insularity of modern homes increasingly takes the form of surveillance or "smart security"'.[3] Through devices such as Ring doorbells, people are made to feel unsafe in their homes unless they can use surveillance technology to pre-emptively distinguish strangers from known people. This way of thinking has become so integrated in our mindset that we might not even notice it anymore.

Since the 1970s, there has been a generalised sense that attempts to house working-class people in state-provided housing have failed. In much of this discourse, public housing estates were presented as the causes of social ills, especially crime and 'antisocial behaviour'. A widespread fear of crime, and the resurgence of a more purely repressive orientation of the state, coincided with a shift in housing policy towards private provision. Critics from the New Right argued that public housing, through its 'paternalist' aim to improve the lives of residents, was in fact doing the exact opposite: creating breeding grounds for maladaptive behaviour and perpetuating slums and poverty. Public housing was seen to have failed because it supposedly failed to produce appropriate social norms and employability.

Jane Jacobs, one of the most influential writers on architecture and cities, argued in her 1961 book *The Death and Life of Great American Cities* that well-used urban streets act as crime deterrents, as frequent use and casual surveillance by the public means that criminals are less likely to get away with crime undetected. For Jacobs, however, safety was merely one aspect of many things that make up a thriving city. The most important thing for her is that cities should be interesting, lively, and diverse. Her dislike of public housing stemmed from a belief that government ownership interferes with the free market and produces aesthetically drab estates, rather than her seeing them primarily as incubators of crime.[4] But in his famous 1972 study *Defensible Space*, architect Oscar Newman used Jacobs' thoughts on visual surveillance and went much further. For Newman, reducing crime on estates was the only consideration. He thought this goal could be achieved by giving people a stake in their immediate surroundings – by creating 'defensible space' that residents would perceive as their own private space. His idea was that this feeling of ownership, even for those who are excluded from legal ownership, would increase communal self-policing of residential areas. At the start of the book, Newman adopted a tone not dissimilar to contemporary police abolitionists, arguing for communities to come together to deal with social problems, rather than outsourcing this function to the police.[5] In Newman's vision, however, the community exists purely in the service of surveillance – sorting neighbours from strangers, and acceptable behaviour from unacceptable infractions. This ideal conservative community serves to impose strict rules for who can enter a space, and what they can do there.

In the mid-1980s, defensible space theory came to England, in the form of Alice Coleman's Thatcherite polemic *Utopia on Trial: Vision and Reality in Planned Housing*. Coleman, a professor at King's College London and the lead researcher of the Design Disadvantagement Team, produced a quasi-scientific condemnation of modern council housing. Like Newman, Coleman used graphs and statistics to give her work scientific authority. But unlike Newman, who used the records of the New York City Housing Authority (which recorded not only rent levels and conditions of dwellings, but also 'family pathology' and crime statistics collected by its own police force), Coleman did not have access to reliable statistics on crime.[6] Instead, she invented the category 'social malaise' to measure just how much estates were failing. But malaise in itself proved quite hard to measure. So Coleman and her collaborators quantified social malaise in terms of six different factors: litter, vandalism, graffiti, number of children placed in care, urine pollution, and faecal pollution.[7] Council housing, she concluded, had failed because it produced publicly visible rubbish and excrement.

For Jacobs, Newman, and Coleman, the underlying problem of publicly owned housing lay in naive and dangerous attempts by the state to interfere with the private market to provide housing, and in particular housing that broke away from the time-honoured tradition of single-family dwellings with sharp demarcations between public and private spheres.

In public housing, they argued, there is a dangerous blurring between public and private, and an inbuilt assumption that people can and should share space and facilities.[8] They thus rejected the most radical legacy of the mid-century public housing programme, arguing that it inevitably led to crime and social malaise. People, they all suggested, cannot and should not share things. From the liberal Jacobs to the reactionary Coleman, there was a consensus that the vision of a more radical form of community that underpinned (some) public housing led to misery for the very people it was designed to help. It therefore needed to be replaced with a conservative form of community – one that rejects shared space but engages in widespread curtain twitching.

The point of this increased emphasis on territoriality and surveillance is to foster a *feeling* of ownership, even for those who are not able to buy their homes. The form of privacy envisioned would seek to mimic traditional forms of home-ownership, but extended to those who have previously been excluded from owning much of anything. This, conservative thinkers hoped, would induce people to reduce their dependence on state authorities and foster self-reliance and independence. Here we can see how an increasingly hegemonic neoliberal form of governance is strongly tied up with forms of subjectivity and a sense of ownership, even as state policies designed to encourage asset ownership can't realistically be extended to most poor people. The working class, in this ideological configuration, must be made to desire a feeling of ownership and privacy. Both Coleman and Newman insisted that working-class people in fact already do desire these things, because the desire for ownership is natural and universal. Newman argued that he was not imposing middle-class social values on working-class people, but instead giving them the chance to realise their innate desire for privacy and security.[9] But in conservative thought, this desire must also be taught to those who haven't yet come to inhabit this supposedly natural subjectivity. Architecture itself can educate this desire. A good fence around a front garden can go a long way towards restoring residents' latent passion for ownership.

Architectural Design and the Fear of Crime

The conservative architectural critique subordinated all other considerations for what good housing is to an overarching concern for crime and bad behaviour. In this, architectural writings reflected a broader social shift towards a more reactionary understanding of society. As fear of crime increased and was fed by political and media narratives on supposedly increasing crime rates, the ideal of good housing was replaced by an ideal of architecture that designed away crime. Jacobs, Newman, and Coleman were all critical of the idea that architecture could create new forms of behaviour and more collective forms of sociality. They argued that this is the naive and mistaken view of utopian authoritarians, who want to use state mechanisms to create broad social change. Architecture, they believed, should only be used to impose existing social norms and discourage deviant behaviour.[10] But they argued against the idea that they were architectural determinists, suggesting instead that architecture can at most influence the behaviour of the majority of people, rather than determining the behaviour of all. As Coleman succinctly put it, some people will always be 'sluts and criminals', even in the most well-designed environments.[11]

The type of crime that troubled Newman and Coleman most was property damage. Indeed, Coleman hardly mentioned violence against persons. Instead, it was vandalism that came to stand in for a broader social disorder. For Newman, vandalism was mainly associated with strangers penetrating the borders of the estate. He thus placed great emphasis on surveillance, not only to impose social control on the estate's residents, but more importantly to separate residents from strangers.[12] If there is one thing that most clearly distinguishes Jacobs' writings from Newman's, it's the role of strangers in crime prevention. For Jacobs, encountering strangers is an inevitable and mostly beneficial aspect of city life.[13] The desire to insulate oneself from strangers is not compatible with the vibrant city life she championed. For Newman, however, strangers should as far as possible be kept away from residential areas. While he argued against spatial segregation and gated communities – suggesting that his defensible space theory could enable crime prevention while creating racially and economically mixed neighbourhoods – he ended up defending a vision of the residential area as a homogeneous and exclusionary enclave within the city.[14] While evoking the racist idea of stranger danger, Newman simultaneously downplayed the large amount of violence that takes place within private spaces, including domestic abuse and sexual assault. He also didn't consider that neighbours sometimes use extensive surveillance as part of racist and sexist harassment, often targeted at those who are seen as 'out of place' within the residential community.

Only some crime, then, registers as a problem for those concerned with increasing domestic security. In its almost exclusive focus on property crimes, defensible space theory foreshadowed broken windows policing, developed in 1990s New York. Both were premised on an assumption that relatively mild forms of property damage or negligent behaviour, such as broken windows or littering, will lead to worse forms of criminal and antisocial behaviour if they go unchallenged.[15] While Newman and Coleman insisted that their self-policing ideal communities would lead to decreased police budgets, their theories were part and parcel of a general shift towards increased policing of 'lifestyle' crime.[16]

This fear of widespread property damage led them to look for forms of domestic architecture that could enable surveillance. Newman also proposed that by extending the private sphere to encompass not only the dwelling itself but its immediate surroundings, residents could be encouraged to see those surroundings as their own and therefore as their responsibility. His main architectural principle was to maximise a sense of territoriality and natural surveillance. Any form of community that arises from these principles was a mere byproduct of the all-important goal of crime deterrence.[17] For Newman, the single-family home, with its own plot of land, was the natural ideal to be emulated in all forms of housing. This type of home was not simply one of many possible forms of housing, but instead represented a stake in the Western social system.[18] Coleman even argued that the single-family semi-detached home represents the instinctual, evolutionary end-point of the human development of shelter.[19] This ideological preference – disguised as scientifically uncovered natural fact – led Coleman and Newman to argue that multi-household dwellings should not have been built, and where it exists it must be modified in order to resemble the suburban house as closely as possible. One of Newman's biggest concerns was fire stairs, which he thought would enable criminals to confound police. Coleman even proposed the removal of the upper floors of buildings taller than three storeys, but admitted that this might not always be a practicable solution. Instead, she suggested that the removal of lifts and multiple staircases might sometimes be a suitable solution, in order to minimise the number of exit routes serving any one home – accessibility and fire safety be damned. Coleman argued that social malaise causes more cases of arson, so fire services should be happy if escape routes were removed.[20] Throughout their writings, the two authors presented a vision of life totally subordinated to the fear of property damage.

In order to minimise crime, this line of thinking suggests, the boundary between public and private must be reinforced. This reinforcement can take both symbolic and physical forms. Estates are dangerous because their design allows an unsettling blurring of private and public spheres. As Daniel Renwick and Robbie Shilliam point out, this critique of public housing echoes nineteenth-century philanthropic concern for urban slums, in which working-class inhabitants failed to replicate appropriate bourgeois distinctions between the domestic sphere and its outside.[21] The deviant working-class behaviours that Jacobs, Newman, and Coleman associated with estates must therefore be fixed by the introduction of clear mechanisms of demarcation. Coleman – momentarily abandoning her distaste for paternalism – further emphasised that the purpose of these fixes must be clearly explained to the residents, lest they persist in their habit of allowing strangers through the newly reinforced barriers surrounding their homes.[22] The new community created by these barriers would function as an antidote to the anonymity produced by large estates, enabling residents to sort neighbours from strangers and undoing the social basis for the neuroses, mental illness, and antisocial behaviour that Coleman claimed are caused by buildings without proper boundaries.[23]

For Newman, the point of sorting strangers from neighbours was also that residents would be more likely to intervene if they saw a neighbour being victimised than if the victim were a stranger. Unlike Jacobs, who assumed that people can and do come to the aid of strangers, Newman suggested that there is a deep apathy stemming from the anonymity of city life, and that this apathy also prevents us from effectively intervening in crimes committed against those we do not know. As an example of this, he mentions the murder of Kitty Genovese in 1964, in which thirty-eight neighbours allegedly heard Genovese scream but failed to call the police.[24] This has since been dubbed 'the bystander effect' – a tendency for people to remain passive observers rather than intervening to stop harm. However, this account of Genovese's murder has since been disproved, as most neighbours didn't hear or see anything, and the few who saw something did take some form of action, even if they failed to prevent Genovese's death.[25] What might be stopping us from intervening, then, is less a feeling of apathy and more a lack of strategies that can ensure the safety of both the victim and those who do intervene. Locating the failure to protect strangers in some eternal human nature – assuming we are only capable of feeling empathy for those we already know – rather than in an absence of social strategies and habits that enable intervention, risks naturalising and perpetuating our lack of concern for the wellbeing of strangers.

The Social Reproduction of Conservative Domesticity

Domestic design does play a role in the reproduction of capitalist society and social relations. This reproduction operates on several levels simultaneously – as the reproduction of the family unit, as the reproduction of class relations, and as the reproduction of the nation state and its racialised order. The socialisation of children is a key concern for conservative thinkers. They locate the root cause of the issues with estates in that the working class is supposedly failing to raise employable children who can become virtuous and productive citizens. Instead, proletarian children are too numerous, too unruly, and too prone to disrespecting private property. As noted in the preceding chapter, there is a fear of the unruly surplus population exceeding their strictly demarcated boundaries. The concentration of children on estates is a key issue for these thinkers, and their increased dispersal among adults would be desirable. As generations have been raised on estates instead of in traditional one-family houses, the adults may themselves lack the appropriate sociability and subjectivity to pass on to their children. Coleman, writing in the mid-1980s, thus felt a sense of urgency to deal with the problem before the generation that were raised in normal homes with normal social values died without having passed on those values to their children and grandchildren.[26]

For the conservative thinkers of architecture, one of the most important functions of the cherished private garden is that it supposedly enables mothers to supervise their children's play, and therefore to intervene if the children do something bad. A clearer boundary between private and public space, Coleman believed, would also teach children to respect the private property of others, and make them less likely to commit acts of vandalism when they are teenagers. Flats, on the other hand, tend to create 'confused space' which is neither public nor private.[27] They also make surveillance of children more difficult. Newman argued that middle-class families may well be able to cope with life in high-rise buildings quite easily, as they have a strong set of values that can be passed on to children, and they also supervise their children more effectively, even if the design of their homes doesn't encourage such surveillance. But for conservative thinkers, 'low-income' and 'welfare' families, especially those with a female head of household, need all the help they can get to break the patterns of dependency and general lack of personal responsibility that structure their lives. Certain social groups (primarily working-class single mothers and their children) are thus more susceptible to bad design.[28]

This emphasis on constant surveillance of one's own children increases the burden on the individual household. In Coleman's own utopia, the socialisation of children is entirely privatised within the nuclear family. This means increasing demands on parental supervision, as any collective form of child-minding, or children spending time unsupervised, is inherently risky. Coleman's desire for children to be supervised by their own parents in private gardens meant that she was against the provision of public play areas within estates. She claimed that residents who said they wanted more play areas were misguided.[29] The ideal number of playgrounds on an estate, according to her schema of design disadvantagement, is zero. This is part of a wider attack on the idea of any shared facilities or amenities near domestic spaces. Since Coleman thought that urine and faecal pollution was such a big issue on estates, it might have been reasonable to suggest building more public toilets in those areas. But Coleman didn't even mention that possibility, which presumably would attract the 'wrong kind of people' and thus create more social malaise. In fact, she advocated the removal of public facilities as far as possible, so that people are forced to meet all their needs within the private household. Children, she suggested, will only become well-adjusted adults if they are cared for within the private household. As Alison Blunt and Robyn Dowling note, over the course of the late twentieth century, there was a shift from understanding the neighbourhood itself as 'home' and thus safe for children to play in, towards a more restrictive understanding in which children are only safe within the space of the domestic household.[30] Tropes of stranger danger therefore serve to perpetuate a culture in which children are less likely to have close contact with a wider range of people outside their families. This arguably leaves them more isolated and likely to be subjected to abuse and violence within the domestic sphere.

But for conservative thinkers, the actual safety of children is at most a marginal concern. The main worry is that proletarian children will grow up to perpetuate a culture of low emotional investment in capitalist social relations. Coleman speculated that poor housing design might even cause widespread unemployment, as lack of parental supervision creates antisocial children with poor educational outcomes, who grow up to become unemployable and maladjusted adults.[31] This familiar trope of cultures of welfare dependency is thus given an architectural basis. Newman was also concerned that old divisions between classes – which enabled people of different social positions to live harmoniously in proximity to one another in the small towns of yore – are becoming too blurred and unstable in the contemporary city. While Jacobs was adamant that the class homogeneity of estates was a key part of the problem, and argued in favour of the now-cherished 'mixed community', Newman suggested that ethnic and class separation might be if not desirable, then at least necessary until order has been restored in cities. Coleman argued that respectable middle-class homeowners could have a stabilising effect on problem areas, but mainly because homeowners are more likely to live in houses rather than flats that produce social malaise.[32]

Either way, the authors agreed that the way we design or modify the housing stock will have profound implications for overall class relations. In an ideal society, working-class and middle-class people will live together, so that social cohesion will prevail. Newman and Jacobs in particular presented their project as a progressive one, which will extend the safety and stability of middle-class life to working-class people, and enable the poor to enjoy the security of a properly territorialised home. They are thus to be brought into society by having a stake in the social order and by sharing social values with their middle-class neighbours. This claim is similar to how the UK Labour Party described their vision of council housing in the 1940s, with the doctor, the grocer, the butcher, and the farm labourer living on the same street.[33] But while Coleman was writing, the Thatcher government was busy changing the social basis for this project. Instead of most people having access to council housing, it became reserved for the very poorest, and the more upwardly mobile could instead buy their council home. Today, many council estates are indeed 'socially mixed', with a large contingent of middle-class private renters paying high rents to live in former council homes. As buildings are still owned by the council, but individual flats are owned by private landlords, responsibility for repair and maintenance is becoming increasingly obscure. But the spread of private ownership has enabled a rejuvenated private rented sector. This is the future the Thatcherites wanted.

The ideas of successful familial and class reproduction are tied up with housing policy as a basis for the continued success of the white, bourgeois nation. The title of Jacobs' book, and indeed the whole intellectual project of defensible space, is premised on a concern for the decay and degeneration of great American cities, and thus of the country as a whole. The challenge for the defensible space theorists is to save the national capitalist project from its own instability, making sure there is enough of a consensus around the arrangement of contemporary capitalism to keep civil peace. Blunt and Dowling point out that the normative assumption of home (understood as both the private domestic sphere and the nation) requires protection to ensure its familiarity and security.[34]

The spectre that haunts these writings is the inner-city riot, an unruly and racialised underclass rising up against the property order and the governmental apparatuses meant to keep them in check. Race is rarely an explicit point in these texts, and any racism of the defensible space project was disavowed by Newman. As with class, Jacobs and Newman saw themselves as extending the security and niceness currently reserved for white people to a racialised underclass, railing against the ills of segregation and racial discrimination. But it is more or less inevitable, given how racist countries such as the US and the UK are, that this line of thinking would be put to use in a racist way. Much like broken windows policing, it doesn't matter how allegedly antiracist its authors are. What matters is that this theory is meant to give people the tools for policing their own neighbourhoods by separating stranger from neighbour, and the notions of the stranger and the criminal are persistently racialised. Newman encouraged people to vigorously challenge strangers about their business in the neighbourhood. It's not difficult to see how this gives people licence to racially target and hurt anyone who is perceived as out of place within the defensible space.

Coleman's very English version of defensible space theory emphasises the link between Englishness and homeownership. She writes that 'the dream of the Englishman's castle' is in the ascendant – meaning that people want private garden space. She correctly identifies the ownership of a semi-detached single-family suburban home as a peculiarly English obsession, while also suggesting that this represents the highest evolutionary stage of human shelter.[35] This is of course not a contradiction if you think the English are the most civilised and evolved people in the world, but for anyone who has visited other European countries, where the urban rich and poor alike are living in flats, it seems like an odd conclusion. Coleman called for the national housing programme to completely stop building flats.[36] Only if more working-class families are housed in 'traditional' homes can the future of the nation be saved.

This naturalisation of the suburban single-family dwelling as a social ideal is not exclusively an idea of the right – it circulates even among those who otherwise disagree with

Thatcher's project of privatising council housing. The right-wing critiques of domestic architecture reappear in a leftist guise in Lynsey Hanley's 2007 book *Estates*. Presented as a critique of modernist council estates from someone who grew up on one, it repeated many of the claims of conservative critics of council housing, including, importantly, that ordinary people want to live in houses with their own private gardens and that public housing should be visually indistinguishable from private housing.[37]

The conservative desire to socialise children properly, through the use of demarcated private property, is premised on a concern that capitalist societies are creating surplus populations that are becoming increasingly detached from participation in the workforce. In the conservative imaginary, whole swathes of society are ensuring their own survival not through honest wage work but through crime and other immoral behaviour. The fear of crime that these theories are based on doesn't necessarily reflect actual instances of violence. But the public sphere has come to be socially defined as a sphere characterised by fear, competition, and stranger danger, rather than potentially one where we support and look after one another. This, in turn, makes the private sphere appear all the more important as a zone of protection and security in a hostile world. As people retreat into the private sphere, and communal facilities that would enable other forms of care are removed, this tendency becomes self-reinforcing. Conservative writings on architecture are thus the perfect supplement to a broader neoliberal ideology that privileges the family over any other form of sociality. It is the family which must be defended (through violence if need be) against both attack by strangers and the risk of its own internal disintegration and degeneration into unruly groupings of single mothers and antisocial children.

Zoe Hu has described a certain desire for a return to traditional gender norms as 'agoraphobic' – denoting a fear of the public space. For women, this marks a complete return to the private sphere of the home. She writes:

> As a concept, 'the family' has worked even harder than 'the individual' to overshadow our ethical obligations to other people. But few have use for notions of society anymore, defined as it is by unpredictability and fear of rising crime. We want only securitized intimacy – the happy assurance of a shared mortgage.[38]

A fear of crime and a desire for heteronormative intimacy thus go hand in hand. Gender is rarely mentioned explicitly by conservative architecture critics. Instead, they take traditional gender relations for granted as natural and therefore good. It is obvious to them that it is mothers who have the overall responsibility to make sure that their children do not commit criminal damage. Alongside a desire to literally rebuild the 'traditional English streetscape',[39] then, is a concomitant but broadly unspoken desire to preserve traditional families and their divisions of labour.

Coleman met Thatcher to discuss defensible space theory, and was given a government grant of £50 million to try out her theories in real life.[40] The project seems to have been fairly unsuccessful, and the reception of Coleman's work has been broadly negative within academia. In the 1970s, social scientists were already criticising Newman for his misuse of statistics to support his theories.[41] However, the fact that these writers had a poor grasp of scientific method did not stop people from reproducing their ideas, as they fit with the new zeitgeist. And perhaps they were partly right in pointing to a link between poor building design and so-called anti-social behaviour, as a lot of the tensions of living near other people could be minimised if the quality of our homes were improved. Disputes between neighbours could, for example, be alleviated by better sound-proofing.[42] The ways we live our lives, and how we interact with others, are shaped by the built environment.

Perhaps there was also a grain of truth to their critique of public landlords. The state has not always been a great provider of homes, and it is true that council bureaucracies often operate in ways that are detrimental to tenants. But in the forty years since Coleman wrote *Utopia on Trial*, it has become abundantly clear that this is not an effect of the social democratic state's more utopian tendencies. Rather, private landlords and housing associations have proved at least as bad as councils. As we have seen, the failure to be responsive to tenants' needs might just be part and parcel of what it means to be a landlord – why carry out improvement to homes when it's easier to do nothing and accept the passive income generated by the ownership of homes? Coleman thought that the private market was more responsive to people's needs and desires than the bureaucratic state.[43] But the rise of private landlordism has broadly shown the opposite to be the case. And today many working-class people are desperate for council housing rather than homes provided by private landlords – a fact that sits uncomfortably with Coleman's belief that only the free market can meet our needs and desires. The conservative theorists' supposedly anti-authoritarian critique of council housing was in itself deeply authoritarian and moralistic. It presumes to know what people want, and argues that certain desires are natural and good. But people seem to want more than what the moralistic free market evangelists are offering.

Feminists have long insisted on a simple truth: the private sphere does not keep us safe. It is misguided to associate safety with privacy. Replacing the redistributive functions of the state with repressive police functions – working hand in hand with a conservative community of curtain twitchers – does not keep us safe. We need other criteria for good housing than the absence of graffiti. Those criteria must also emphasise the ability of good housing to foster broader life worlds than the private sphere, with all its labour and violence. Feelings of safety and control over one's domestic space do not need to be associated with the privatised and securitised space of the family home, reserved for intimate family members. We can only get free together.

6

Inheriting the Family Home

The family, we often hear, is in crisis. Younger generations, stuck in barely affordable rental accommodation, are waiting to have children, if they are having them at all. This story is often told as a generational one. Because of the baby boomers' supposed hoarding of housing, millennials are now priced out of homeownership and stuck in an increasingly expensive private rental sector. This generational drama is captured in the term Generation Rent – a generation defined by its failure to become homeowners.

Generational Wealth

What the Generation Rent narrative obscures is that the same housing wealth that some baby boomers have attained is being transferred to their children, making this dynamic primarily one of class rather than generation. While this transfer of wealth has been slowed down because of increasingly long lives in the parent generation and inheritances that come later in the lives of their children, it can be sped up by various forms of *inter vivos* transfers – gifts and other forms of financial support that take place while parents are still alive. Home-owning parents provide deposits, use their homes as securities for their children's mortgages, or let children live in the family home while they save money to buy a home of their own. For some people, family wealth – transmitted in the form of inheritance of a house or gifted money for a deposit – becomes a ticket to a more economically secure future. For others, especially those whose parents are renting or live in smaller homes, these forms of support are unavailable. Homeownership becomes more attractive as expensive and insecure private rents eat up more and more of younger people's income, but simultaneously increasingly unattainable as house prices rise. Many younger adults whose parents aren't homeowners have to fend for themselves in an increasingly hostile housing market.

Housing wealth is thus intimately tied up with family relationships. The changes to the housing market, the rental market, and generational wealth transfers are deeply intertwined. The family home is often a place of intimate relationships, and where much of daily life takes place. It can also be a site of ownership and accumulation. These two functions are not necessarily contradictory, as many contemporary housing theorists seem to suggest. In fact, they often go hand in hand. The family and its home, always important economic units rather than merely sentimental connections or psychological bonds, can literally act as securities for a mortgage. Generational wealth transfers increasingly determine not only access to housing, but overall economic security, social status, and health.[1] Anglo-American capitalism has long privileged homeownership over renting, through state subsidies in the form of lower taxation. But as renting became less accessible and affordable and homeownership was sold as an attractive investment opportunity, it became increasingly difficult to access homeownership unless one had access to familial wealth transfers.

The Generation Rent narrative does not fully explain rented accommodation as a complementary housing market, rather than just a place where people live while they wait to become homeowners. For the baby boomer generation, renting was more accessible, affordable, and attractive, as many people had access to lifetime secure rented tenancies. Being a renter for life was not necessarily a problem in itself. The Generation Rent narrative suggests that more people in the millennial generation are renters, and that this in itself is problematic. But just because buying a house is more expensive now does not mean fewer people overall are homeowners. While generational disparities clearly exist, the main problem is not necessarily renting in itself but increasingly exploitative forms of private renting, as well as decreased access to public housing.

For many people, homeownership becomes increasingly unattainable but simultaneously more attractive as house prices increase and private rents eat up more and more of their income. The price of buying a home cannot be separated from the price inflation in the private rented sector, which encourages landlords to buy up homes and drive up costs for other buyers.[2] There is thus a vicious cycle in which increasing rent levels make homeownership more desirable but also more unaffordable. Generational transfers from parents who support their children in getting onto the 'property ladder' therefore coexist with a different form of transfer, in which mostly older landlords derive their income from mostly younger private renters. These transfers are complementary and tend to reinforce existing class divisions, so that people who already own property can use it to create further financial security for themselves and their families. In fact, some people become landlords in order to support adult children or to make sure that their children will have a bigger inheritance, thus using family bonds as a reason to exploit others.

For this system to work – for assets in the form of housing to continue to increase in value – homeownership has to be continually reinforced as the most desirable form of tenure. These processes are both ideological and material. Renting must not just be stigmatised socially, but also made into an objectively worse form of tenure. As we have seen, the Housing Act 1988 massively reduced access to secure and affordable rented accommodation in the UK, as private renters are no longer protected by rent controls and can be evicted without any reason. Similar dynamics operate in countries like the US, where publicly owned rented accommodation has always been reserved for the very poorest households. Not only is homeownership sold as desirable in itself, associated with adulthood and being a respectable citizen, but public housing has been made inaccessible to most people and private renting has become nightmarishly bad.

This dynamic didn't arise with neoliberalism. Throughout the twentieth century, homeownership served as a marker of both the good life and the successful family unit. This was especially the case in countries like the US, where private provision of housing was encouraged by the state. Along with this symbolic function, it was a way of tying increasingly large groups of people to capitalist imperatives of wage labour, as mortgage holders and outright homeowners have a stake in the stability of capitalist economies. Dolores Hayden writes that in the 1920s US, the promotion of homeownership became a way of encouraging social peace and discouraging strikes. Having a literal and symbolic investment in continued mortgage payments meant that the skilled working class became more likely to want steady employment, and thus served as a way of disciplining labour.[3] The ideal of suburban homeownership was also deeply gendered, as the home became a space for relaxation for the male worker but a sphere of unwaged labour for a majority of women. The home functioned as the core commodity to contain other commodities – not only did the family have to buy its own home, but it also had to fill it with domestic appliances and goods supporting leisure and comfort.

Neoliberalism and Housing as Asset

But while homeownership has always been privileged in capitalist economies, its ideological justification has changed somewhat in recent decades. Lorna Fox O'Mahony and Louise Overton point to a shift in terms of how people relate to their housing. Up until the 1980s, they argue, people were simply told that homeownership was a superior tenure form because it offered security and a sense of pride in one's home. They cite a 1971 UK government white paper which states that homeownership 'satisfies a deep natural desire on the part of the householder to have independent control of the home that shelters him and his family. It gives him the greatest possible security against the loss of his home; and particularly against the price changes that may threaten his ability to keep it.'[4] But more recent iterations of the political valorisation of homeownership have emphasised that a home is an asset that can be used for financial security and to buy access to social care. While the social valorisation of homeownership has remained or even increased in the past fifty years, the political justification for this preference has thus shifted to emphasise the role of housing in buying access to services to meet needs other than housing itself.

While this shift has sometimes been presented as one of asset democratisation – giving access to homeownership to almost everyone in society – the effect has been to reinforce existing class divisions. But as Lisa Adkins, Melinda Cooper, and Martijn Konings argue, the idea of homeownership for everyone served an important political function, extending the promise of security to people of all classes and justifying the transition to an austerity model of the welfare state.[5] While the actual experience of housing security was mostly reserved for the middle and upper classes, the story of homeownership democratisation ensured that there were broad constituencies with an interest in maintaining increasing asset prices. Policies that had previously almost exclusively benefitted the bourgeoisie now came to appeal to a much wider social configuration.[6]

As part of the neoliberal regime, there was a shift towards asset-based welfare, wherein previously state-provided services have to be paid for, sometimes out of pension savings or housing wealth. Access to decent-quality childcare and eldercare became more contingent on having savings or housing wealth to draw on. In this discourse, homes become equity – an ever-increasing pot of money that can be mobilised to complement pensions and pay for reproductive services. Once the mortgage is paid off, the house can be remortgaged if needed. Homeownership thus becomes not only a form of protection from eviction and exploitative and negligent landlords, but also a form of financial security and social insurance. But the whole enterprise hinges on the idea that everyone's housing wealth will continue to increase. In the US, Spain, Ireland, and other countries particularly affected by repossessions in the aftermath of the global financial crisis of 2008, this imaginary of housing wealth as secure and ever increasing was revealed as fictional. But the association between homeownership, security, and access to care has not gone away. It is continually being propped up by a political system that is unwilling to provide reproductive services in a collective way, opting instead to privatise social security through homeownership.

The shift towards housing wealth being increasingly important for accessing at least a minimally comfortable life is thus deeply intertwined with the retrenchment of the welfare state. As the state shifted its capacities and resources towards increasingly punitive forms of service provision and surveillance, the responsibility for reproduction became increasingly individualised. If a previous version of the capitalist state had sought to complement a white and heteronormative family model with more widely accessible provision of care, now an increasingly fragmented and insecure family structure had to bear the brunt of capitalist restructuring. And those who are excluded from family and/or housing wealth are encouraged to aspire to the very form of familial homeownership that has served to limit their access to reproductive services. As homeownership emerges as a privatised investment that can be used to fund security and access to care, other forms of social provision can be stripped away with less outrage from the general public. While a lot of people are worse off because of the current organisation of the things people need to live decent lives, wealth and access to life's necessities have supposedly been democratised through widespread homeownership.

The higher levels of homeownership of recent decades were funded through a massive expansion in the access to mortgage debt. As Melinda Cooper shows in her book *Family Values*, in the post-war era US, access to mortgages was closely linked to normative social standards such as stable employment and marital status. This mainly benefitted white, married middle-class and skilled working-class heterosexual couples, while people of colour, single women, queer people, and those with insecure employment status were largely excluded and relegated to the rented sector. Mortgages thus served to reinforce a normative family order, but many people could access homeownership without having access to familial wealth. As access to mortgages was 'democratised' from the 1990s onwards, marginalised people were seemingly included in the prosperity promised by homeownership.[7] But as house prices have continued to rise, access to inheritances, *inter vivos* transfers, or other forms of familial support have become increasingly central to access to housing security. Changes to taxation in many European and North American countries also meant that it has become cheaper to transfer wealth through families, either as gifts or as inheritance.[8] For those who don't have access to familial wealth, homeownership becomes harder to access. And while homeownership increased in many European and North American countries in the 1980s, 1990s, and early 2000s, homeownership rates in the US and the UK are now lower than twenty years ago.[9]

The function of asset ownership, then, is not so much to fundamentally change how class lines are drawn. Rather, homeownership has broadly tended to reinforce existing class divisions that are derived from the sphere of production and waged work. While some working-class people who had previously been excluded from homeownership were included through laxer mortgage regulations, the global financial crisis meant that in many countries these people were also likely to lose their homes through foreclosure. The increased importance of intra-family wealth transfers for access to housing has meant that class divisions tend to be reproduced rather than disrupted.[10] In Cooper's account, feminist and antiracist struggles over state provision of services and benefits in the 1960s and 1970s meant that, for a brief moment, the welfare state was undermining the heterosexual nuclear family and enabling a decent quality of life outside of normative familial forms. As the state shifted its focus to encouraging more marginalised people to access homeownership, however, it simultaneously reinforced 'the tyranny of family wealth' by making sure that people needed access to some form of familial support to access mortgages. It also meant that newly asset-rich constituencies such as middle-class gay and lesbian people had an interest in the state legibility of their familial forms, to ensure that their wealth was passed on to the right people when they die. Civil partnership, marriage, and adoption rights rose to the top of the LGBT civil rights agenda at the same time as gay people were increasingly construed as ideal mortgage customers.[11]

There are therefore several ways in which homeownership interacts with the organisation of familial units. On the one hand, increased house prices might mean postponing family formation or make it more difficult, as many people in their twenties and thirties struggle to afford enough domestic space and housing security to have children. Of course, many poorer households do have children, but younger middle-class households hold off on having children in order to minimise a drop in living standards due to expensive childcare and the need for more domestic space.

On the other hand, homeownership strengthens the family in various ways. Crucially, it reinforces the bonds of dependency between adult children and their parents, as young adults are staying in their parental homes for longer.[12] These relationships are also important for *inter vivos* transfers, through which ageing parents leverage their relative security to alleviate the precarious housing situation of their children. These transfers can also reinforce a sense of emotional obligation towards family members. *Inter vivos* transfers may impose an expectation that adult children should support their parents in their old age, and research shows that recipients of familial gifts tend to live closer to their parents and spend more time with them. But these transfers also create a norm that the recipients should provide financial support for their own children once they reach adulthood.[13] Homeownership and its attendant aspirations and obligations can therefore serve to reinforce familial bonds not only between parents and their children but over several generations.

Homeownership can also increase the importance of romantic coupledom, as two people can more easily access housing security than a single person. Renters and homeowners alike have an incentive to share a room or a house with a partner, to split the ever-increasing cost of housing. Married or cohabiting couples also have easier access to mortgages and therefore to homeownership. Capitalist states have also typically offered various tax benefits to married couples. This might incentivise women in particular, who generally have a weaker economic position than men, to aspire to stable relationships which promise to provide emotional, financial, and housing security. It can also disincentivise divorce, as marital dissolution tends to lead to worse housing outcomes.[14] While mortgages are less explicitly tied to marriage than they were in the post-war era, the economic pressure of housing costs implicitly favours romantic partnership over living as a single person.

The vicious cycle in the housing market means that rent and house prices mutually reinforce one another. The attractiveness of homeownership is in many ways connected to the instability and insecurity of the private rented sector. At the same time, increasing house prices mean that many people who want to own their homes can't afford to buy, and are instead stuck in the private rented sector.[15] This generalised feeling of insecurity increases the sense of importance of attaining homeownership, and means that homeownership becomes exclusively associated with a feeling of safety. Even those who are unlikely to ever achieve full ownership of a home, and may spend all their lives paying either a private landlord or a bank, are made to invest emotionally in the idea of homeownership as the achievement of security. As Adkins, Cooper, and Konings point out, Margaret Thatcher understood this emotional appeal of investment in homeownership as a source of stability.[16] This investment also creates a sense of participation in and attachment to capitalist economies more broadly, as the mortgager or homeowner's economic stability becomes tied up with general asset price inflation. We need to understand ownership not only as economic investment, but as a structure of feeling – one that shapes the aspirations and emotional investments of both homeowners and renters.

Karl Marx and Friedrich Engels understood property ownership and inheritance as one of the core functions of the bourgeois family form.[17] Since the nineteenth century, this function has been increasingly generalised across classes. It's no longer only the upper classes who have access to property, but many middle-class wage earners as well. It is often through homeownership that people form an emotional investment in the continued success of capitalist housing markets. What for some people feels like a housing crisis can for others be a story of economic success and prosperity. Homeowners, then, have a stake in the continuation of the current housing system and the continued exploitation of private renters. The individualising discourses around housing, which makes access to good housing into a personal responsibility, can also mean that housing wealth can feel like a personal achievement – a savvy investment at the right time and the wise management of familial resources, rather than the result of structural changes to capitalist economies.

While discourses about the family being in crisis have been rife over the last few decades, homeownership is one of the ways in which the family form retains its grip on our lives. Lindsay Flynn and Herman Mark Schwartz write that societal processes of de-familialisation have been increasingly replaced with re-familialisation over recent decades, as economic insecurity and welfare state retrenchment mean that more people have to pool social and economic risk within their family units.[18] This new version of the family might be less stable over the course of a lifetime than the post-war nuclear family, as people postpone partnership and having children, and are more likely to get divorced and remarried. But despite the laments about the family's decline, homeownership is deeply intertwined with normative ideals about personal responsibility, familial bonds, and domestic security. Family, then, becomes inscribed in the built environment not only through architecture but also through forms of ownership that perpetuate class and normative kinship structures. As family and ownership are deeply imbricated, the positive associations of family are conflated with private property. And in this way, homeownership becomes simultaneously a means of providing housing security for one's family and a form of attachment to capitalist society.

7

Demanding More, Demanding Better

Should we, then, simply build more public housing? The council home stands as a symbol of the affordability and security of tenure that has largely been lost in the UK since the 1980s. The UK's turn to market solutions to the housing question was followed by many other countries, and it has largely caused the situation that we're in today – high rents, frequent evictions, homes riddled with disrepair. In this situation, a return to a previous and more equitable housing system seems tempting. Private sector housing is increasingly unaffordable for many people, especially in the large cities where many have to live to find work. In response, the UK government created the category of 'affordable housing', which is generally understood to be any form of housing (renting, homeownership, or a mix of the two) that costs 80 per cent or less of market price. However, as average wages have failed to keep up with average rents and house prices, this is still out of reach for most. Other categories purport to offer 'genuinely affordable rent', such as the London Living Rent scheme. While such categories proliferate, they fail to meet the needs of most working-class people.

Non-profit housing associations, meanwhile, have become increasingly commercialised. Some of them can trace their lineage to nineteenth-century philanthropic associations, which were largely formed to improve the conditions of slum-dwelling working-class people, while also securing a comfortable 5 per cent profit for their investors. These organisations have a long history of paternalistic attempts to 'improve' their tenants as well as their housing conditions. Octavia Hill was a well-known reformer whose methods aimed to produce a more well-behaved working class, focusing especially on turning working-class women into respectable people who could adhere to strict rules and would always prioritise paying their rent on time.[1] Other housing associations were created in the twentieth century as more local and community-based attempts to provide housing. But in the shift towards market provision of housing, housing associations were increasingly privileged over council housing. They were seen as unencumbered by the bureaucratic inefficiency associated with the local state. This shift was initiated by the Thatcher government, but continued by New Labour. The Decent Homes Programme, notionally introduced in order to improve the social housing stock, tied funding for the compulsory upgrade to three options: transfer of the council's housing stock to a housing association, using a Private Finance Initiative (PFI), or creating an Arms-Length Management Organisation (ALMO).[2] This shift meant that the state strongly encouraged the privatisation of its own housing stock, making it almost impossible for local authorities to retain management of their own housing while also having the funds to maintain their properties. Nationally, about half of council housing has been transferred to housing associations, which are nominally non-profit. But, as funding from central government has been sharply reduced, they rely on loans from private finance institutions, and therefore have to behave *as if* they were private companies to maintain the confidence of their lenders and keep up with their interest payments.[3] While housing associations don't produce profit for shareholders, then, they do produce profits for their lenders.

Local authorities themselves have increasingly engaged in marketised management of their housing stock. This shift had to be forced upon some councils, but was greeted with enthusiasm by others. As central government funding and loans for building and maintaining council housing have been dramatically reduced, councils too have turned to private finance. Stuart Hodkinson has vividly described the disastrous effect of PFIs – a state-imposed system through which councils have outsourced part of their activity to private consortiums, paying a lot of money to receive typically substandard services in return. In the context of housing, PFIs led to dangerous 'improvements' to the housing stock, while at the same time obfuscating responsibility for repair and maintenance.[4]

Another option that some councils have used over the past years, ostensibly to circumvent state restrictions on local authority borrowing and building, is setting up a council-owned Special Purpose Vehicle (SPV), which allows councils to act as private developers. While Labour councils have argued that they have set up SPVs to create housing for those who can't afford private rents, Joe Beswick and Joe Penny have observed that the operating practices of council-owned SPVs are entirely borrowed from the world of private companies, and councils are increasingly using their land as financial assets.[5] This often means demolishing existing council estates and replacing them with 'mixed communities', so that councils can generate income from private rents and the sale of homes. Extensive regeneration programmes, whether using SPVs or simply working with private developers, have typically led to much higher densities on the sites of former council estates, but with a loss of many social homes and the displacement of former residents.[6]

Given the state of the housing system as we know it, the call to build more council housing makes sense. It is a demand for renewed state investment in decent housing – something we all depend on to ensure a good quality of life, and from which low-income people are increasingly excluded. Rather than seeing council homes sold off or demolished, the housing movement is calling for reinvestment in public housing, which exists to serve as homes, not financial assets.

But this seemingly simple slogan – build more council homes – is based on an assumption that council housing means essentially one thing, and that we all want the same *type* of council housing. This is despite the fact that, as housing historian Michael Harloe points out, the history of state-owned housing is full of contradictory purposes and models of housing provision. Harloe distinguishes different models of state-provided housing. Mass housing sought to provide state-owned homes for a broad section of the population, whereas the residual model limited access to publicly owned homes to those who could not afford to rent or buy on the private market. He also mentions the communally owned and managed form of housing, but notes that this version of social housing has never been dominant in any capitalist country.[7]

Many proponents of council housing also fall prey to what David Madden and Peter Marcuse refer to as 'the myth of the benevolent state' – the idea that the state intervenes in housing simply in order to provide high-quality homes for the masses. Instead, Madden and Marcuse suggest that state intervention often stems from a desire to preserve the existing order.[8] But today, critiques of some forms of council housing are usually dismissed by many on the left – any negative aspect of state-provided housing is seen as a result of Tory government austerity programmes that have aimed to shrink the state. The aim of the housing movement, in this narrative, should be to restore the welfare state to its former glory, so that once again it can undertake large-scale construction of publicly owned homes. For example, John Boughton writes:

> Grenfell has reminded us, in the most powerful way imaginable, how much we need the state. We need its regulation and oversight to protect us from commercially driven agendas which value profit over people. We need its investment to provide the safe, secure and affordable housing for all that the market never will. And we need its idealism – that aspiration to treat all its citizens equitably and decently which lay at the very heart of the council house building programme which improved the lives of many millions of our citizens from the 1890s.[9]

In a similar vein, Vicky Spratt argues that housing is the responsibility of the state, and that this represents a 'politics of love'. For Spratt, grassroots struggles for better housing are merely doing work that ought to be done by the state, and are therefore enabling and maintaining the current system.[10] But contrary to Boughton, even if we were to bracket the use of the inherently exclusionary category 'citizen', it has never been the case that the state has been committed to treating everyone equitably. And whatever 'idealism' or 'love' the state has displayed is usually the result of class struggle rather than some inherent willingness on the state's part to protect people from the ravages of the market. The idea that we could simply return to council housing as a common sense position across the political spectrum erases how the working class has had to fight for decent housing, rather than it being a gift from a benevolent state.

This is not to say that council housing has never improved people's lives. The best council housing is high-quality, spacious, and beautiful, and gives residents access to facilities and community resources. It enabled a more communal life and minimised the amount of rent that working-class tenants had to hand over in exchange for housing. While it would be misleading to argue that this is a fully decommodified form of housing, council rents can be used for the maintenance of homes rather than going into the pockets of landlords. As noted in the introduction, councils have sometimes acted to prevent gentrification by buying up properties that have been neglected by private landlords, and then repairing them and transforming them into cheaper council housing.[11] As the climate crisis makes it increasingly unsustainable to build large numbers of new homes, this could be an important programme to learn from in our current time. Even better, councils could simply take over vacant or neglected properties. Expropriating private landlords would be a massive step forwards in the contemporary housing struggle.

But, as Sita Balani points out, the welfare state is highly ambiguous, as its practices are 'informed by multiple, sometimes competing rationales'. It is therefore 'neither inherently oppressive nor liberatory'.[12] The call for more council housing, then, must be mindful of this ambiguity of the state. We must be more specific in terms of what types of housing – council-owned or otherwise – we actually want and need. Council housing comes in many different forms, and they are not all equal.

Without the state intervening in social reproduction, capitalism would not be able to sustain itself. The welfare state is a particular form of state intervention, which aims to ensure the reproduction of labour power by providing free or cheap education, healthcare, childcare, housing, and so on. This can also be understood as a class compromise between workers and capital – capitalists agree to higher taxation of profits to ensure that the state can provide the services workers need to live a reasonably dignified and healthy life. These welfare provisions, including low rents, can also be a way to stem demands for higher wages. The working class, however, has not always been pacified by this deal. In the late 1960s, at the height of the welfare era, there was widespread unrest and demands for more than the state and capital were offering.

Because of the ambiguous status of the welfare state, we need to look more carefully at how the state intervenes in the reproduction of capitalist societies. This involves an analysis of social reproduction – all the activities that go into maintaining the lives, wellbeing, and skills of workers – as not something external to capitalist relations but part of capitalism itself. Specifically to housing, the state can adapt its policies around the design of homes, their quality and size, their allocation and the inclusion or exclusion of certain groups, and the rules and regulations that apply to council tenants. While 'council housing' appears as one coherent object in a lot of left discourse, what council housing is and how it functions has varied. Its purpose has also been dependent on who is designing and implementing those policies.

There is a widespread idea that there was a pre-Thatcherite consensus between the Tories and Labour to build council housing, and that such a consensus should be restored.[13] But the history of council housing is much more complicated and varied. Post-war Tory and Labour governments alike were committed to the principle of building more council homes, but the standards and types of homes being built were always contested. Paul Watt argues that the idea of a post-war consensus is somewhat mythical, as there were constantly shifting standards and rationales for state intervention in housing. He also highlights the long-standing Tory commitment to homeownership, expressed in local Right to Buy policies that predated the national Thatcherite policy by several decades.[14] For the Tories, council housing was only ever a type of housing intended for poor people who couldn't afford to buy their home. This version of council housing did little to challenge the general respect for private property that underpins capitalist societies. Instead, it merely acted as a complement to private markets. Harloe points out that the

Labour Party, especially from the early 1970s onwards, was also deeply committed to this vision of homeownership as the standard form of housing provision, with council housing playing a purely complementary function. In this context, he writes, the Labour government of 1974–79 imposed controls on local authority spending, which laid the groundwork for the more drastic attacks on council housing once Thatcher was in power.[15]

Labour governments in the immediate post-war era did espouse a vision of more generalised provision of council housing, but even this vision has never encompassed everyone. Daniel Renwick and Robbie Shilliam argue that the only real consensus on council housing that existed during the post-war years was that the white and respectable working class should be given access to it, rather than unruly members of the surplus population.[16] Allocation policies and practices, whether legal or informal, have always sought to distinguish between those who are deserving of council housing and those who are not. These judgements have often been based on categories such as citizenship and length of residency, as well as housing officers' attitudes to different groups of tenants.[17] While the Labour Party at some points in its history has been committed to the idea of council housing for most people (the middle class as well as the working class), it has never embraced a fully equitable allocation of homes. Council housing up until the early 1970s was mainly distributed to the white, heterosexual, employed working class.[18] It thus typically excluded migrants, the unemployed, and other members of the surplus population. Balani writes that welfare services have been used to consolidate the distinction between citizen and non-citizen – 'casting racialised outsiders as a drain on national services' – while also disciplining service recipients into good reproductive subjects.[19] Similarly, Shilliam argues that housing officers have sometimes positioned themselves as the guardians of state resources, protecting them against those racialised subjects seen as incapable of caring for publicly owned properties.[20]

Throughout much of its history, including what most regard as the golden age of council housing, the allocation of homes has contributed to the sorting of people into different sectors of the working class, and therefore also to the working class's fragmentation. For much of the twentieth century, migrants and racialised citizens were concentrated in slum-like conditions in the private rented sector. In the context of Bengali migrants living in London's East End, Shabna Begum writes that even when these households were offered council housing, they were given a narrower and inferior range of options.[21] Adah Kaye, Marjorie Mayo, and Mike Thompson write that the local state has never been willing to accept responsibility for housing everyone, and that it has been especially unwilling to house the migrant workers who live in the country for a few years before returning to their home countries.[22] It was not until council housing was already being starved of resources that it was opened up to a wider segment of the population. Changes to law made in the 1970s meant that the racialised surplus population was now being housed in council estates that were beginning to deteriorate, rather than the shoddy private housing they had previously been confined to. Whether housed by the state or by private landlords, then, migrants and racialised members of the surplus population have often been relegated to the worst housing.

While some council housing was well built, a lack of funds often meant that councils were skimping on quality. The Parker Morris Standards, the nationwide building standards introduced in 1963, stipulated that councils had to build bigger homes. But Kaye, Mayo and Thompson write that these higher standards, in combination with funding cuts, resulted in councils using cheaper building materials.[23] Over time, this meant higher costs for repairs – money that increasingly cash-strapped councils did not have. Things got worse during austerity, and a lack of funding for basic maintenance meant that council estates were allowed to deteriorate.[24] As noted in chapter 4, this coincided with increasing social stigmatisation, as the media and politicians were conflating poor standards with the subjectivity of the residents.

In the US, the history of state-funded housing has been somewhat different than in the UK and some other European countries, as it never existed as housing available to both middle-class and working-class households. Here, public housing was always residualised. It was intended only for the very poorest and in no way allowed to compete with private provision of homes.[25] Apart from during times of national crisis – for example when there has been a need to build mass housing for workers in war-time industries – the US state has mainly supported private markets through subsidised mortgages and tax subsidies rather than directly producing homes.[26] Somewhat ironically, this meant that the Reagan government couldn't follow the Thatcher government's lead when it came to privatisation, as the US public housing stock was of such poor quality and design that it wasn't attractive to buy, either for would-be homeowners or for institutional landlords.[27]

But even properly funded and designed council housing has not been without flaws. Red Vienna, with its large-scale municipal house-building programme that took place 1919–34, is often upheld as an example of the best council housing. There are many things to admire about this project – a genuine commitment to building decent homes for the working class, very low rents (on average 4 per cent of wages), and extensive communal facilities as well as homes. The Viennese local government introduced strict rent controls, which meant that private landlordism became unprofitable. This in turn reduced land values, with the result that the city could buy land cheaply. Semi-public shared space for residents meant that they had access to communal laundries, play areas, and parks.[28] As with elsewhere, this now almost unthinkable state intervention was not simply handed to the people of Vienna; popular discontent was growing following World War I, and decent housing was necessary to stave off a Bolshevik-inspired uprising. Because of this, architectural historian Eve Blau describes Red Vienna as a social democratic attempt to ward off the threat of both communism and fascism, and preserve aspects of liberal democracy while working towards socialism.[29] As such, this housing also incorporated elements which reproduced capitalist social relations, for example by keeping wages low and maintaining a healthy workforce, alongside its more radical and collective aspirations. Even here, then, we can see the deeply ambiguous qualities of state-provided housing under capitalism.

The ideal of the nuclear family model underpinned much of the overarching project of Red Vienna, often contrary to the Viennese working class's more loose and open household arrangements. Thus, many residents came to experience the Red Vienna project as a paternalistic imposition of bourgeois ideals and behaviours. And while the architects of Red Vienna paid some attention to reproductive labour and sought to communalise it, this work was still assumed to be women's responsibility. Blau notes that men were banned from using the communal laundries, ostensibly to protect women's privacy – but the laundry attendants were all men.[30]

Similar to council housing in the UK, Red Vienna's housing allocation policy privileged citizens and married couples over others.[31] According to Susanne Soederberg, this legacy is present in Red Vienna's post-war successor, the Vienna model of social housing, which excluded non-citizens until 2006 and still makes it harder for migrants to access housing.[32] Red Vienna also calls into question the frequently made claim that council housing is inherently a more democratic form of housing. While Red Vienna estates had building committees consisting of residents, these were merely advisory, and policies were decided centrally. These policies included the strict rules of behaviour that tenants had to adhere to.[33]

There are similarities to the history of council housing in the UK. Early council housing was designed to encourage respectable, patriarchal, and industrious households.[34] Post-war Labour policy for house-building prioritised building three-bedroom homes and promised a self-contained house for every family who wanted one. A few decades later, the Parker Morris Standards were based on a normative understanding of domestic space, and most homes were designed for nuclear family units.[35] The Parker Morris design guidelines also included 'scenarios' for architects that encouraged them to design kitchens for an imagined housewife who constantly needed to keep an eye on children while also maintaining the kitchen as her exclusive domain.[36]

Today, the proponents of council housing cast it as (at least potentially) more democratically managed than housing association ownership, as housing associations such as Clarion (the UK's biggest landlord) are run increasingly like private businesses with little consideration for the needs of tenants. But it is naive to assume that councils, because they are elected, are inherently more accountable. This seems to be based on wishful thinking about the potential of substantial democratic control of local government. It is thus questionable whether council housing offers an inherently more democratic form of housing. Don Watson argues that even the post-war Labour government, often taken as the best version of the UK state, saw the working class as passive recipients of welfare policies.[37] Even in this iteration of state-provided housing, then, we should not assume that it was intended to be democratically managed. And while councillors are nominally subjected to some pressure to keep residents (in their capacity as voters) happy, this pressure is often in practice quite minimal, as many local authorities function as one-party states and participation in local elections is low. Moreover, councils tend to have a complex bureaucracy which is controlled by unelected officers, not councillors. Many council tenants describe an experience of being ignored for years by their landlord, while living in appalling conditions. In order to make housing more democratic, we would need not just a shift towards council housing but a much more fundamental change in how society works and how local democracy operates.

Today, there seems to be a renewed interest in building social housing, on both the left and the right. However, this does not necessarily signal a shift in the *role* of state intervention in the housing sector. It is increasingly obvious that the private sector can't meet the needs of the very poorest households, and these households often end up in temporary accommodation provided by private landlords but paid for by the state. This model is clearly not working. But calls to provide social housing for this specific group of people mean sustaining a residual model of public housing, rather than challenging the consensus that the market should provide housing for the majority of people.

A core problem with the demand to build more council housing is that much existing council housing is not good. While some of its problems are the result of underfunding, which could be reversed if there were willingness from the government, some of them are more fundamental – built into the very design of the homes and how they have been allocated. The argument that council housing makes economic sense, because it would reduce the costs of housing benefits going into the pockets of UK landlords,[38] also ignores how much of the UK economy is reliant on the private housing market, including the private rented sector. The pro-council housing argument that local governments can make money from the housing they own – which they can then reinvest in other parts of their services – should similarly be rejected, as it is a form of regressive taxation.

Harloe points out that, unlike education and healthcare, housing has never been fully decommodified in capitalist societies, as doing so would challenge the very idea of private property. The residual version of social housing provision has thus been the norm.[39] The tendency in the housing movement to posit a bad market against a good state means that there is often a failure to theorise the state as a *capitalist* state, which is tasked with reproducing capitalism. Even a renewed emphasis on mass provision of council housing, then, wouldn't necessarily go far enough, unless it were to start seriously undermining the view that private property is a core aspect of a good society.

We should avoid embracing 'council housing' *tout court*, and start to recognise that this form of housing has never fully met the needs of everyone. Instead, we could start from an exploration of *what kinds* of housing (council-owned or otherwise) we actually want and need. This must include the needs and desires of those who have been at best precariously included in the council housing project as we know it. Rather than affirming council housing as the end goal of the housing movement, we can see it as a partial and inherently ambiguous improvement of the current housing system. It is also one among several less privatised forms of ownership that could enable residents to have more control over their housing. Creating more council housing is necessary. But so is creating other forms of collectively owned or managed housing – including housing co-ops and democratically managed and small-scale community housing associations. None of these models are perfect in themselves, and none can end the current housing crisis, but together they enable more choice and a greater sense of invention and exploration of new housing forms. Truly public housing must be able to meet the needs of its residents. It must be democratically managed, and it must provide high-quality space, both private and communal. It should not be used to consolidate hierarchies and divisions within the working class. This kind of housing has never existed – it is up to us to fight for it.

8

Collective Housing and the Abolition of the Family

In capitalist society, care is scarce. It is reserved for particular spheres, such as the domestic sphere of the family and institutional settings created by the state. It is also conditional – one must be a member of a family, have citizenship of the right nation, or have a lot of money in order to access care.

Marxist feminists have long argued that this privatisation of care goes hand in hand with the capitalist economy. Bourgeois society instituted a strict social and symbolic division between the domestic sphere and the public sphere, and made provision of care the responsibility primarily of women. While this separation between domestic and public has never been complete, there is typically a lack of care outside of the private home. This also makes it more important to be part of a family, given that it is one of few settings where individuals can access care under capitalism. And all of us need care – the young, the old, the sick and disabled, but also healthy adults. We cannot satisfy all of our needs on our own, especially our emotional needs for safety and intimacy. And the healthy and able-bodied could become sick or disabled, as no one is exempt from the vulnerabilities that come with being a living being. The family functions as an economic unit of redistribution too, so that family members share money and resources. Those who are excluded from the waged economy – because of unemployment, illness, caring responsibilities, or age – often can't survive on benefits and state-provided reproductive services alone, and rely on waged family members for support.

But the family is also a site of intense exploitation, violence, and alienation. Few families could be described as unqualifiedly happy social units. Most people go through difficulties in their family relations at one point or another, and many end up cutting ties with one or several family members. Even when families are working well, the privatisation of care under capitalism puts an enormous amount of strain on them, as they are made to fulfil a broad range of caring responsibilities. This is particularly true of families with young children or individuals with long-term illnesses or disabilities, which are typically left to fend for themselves rather than receiving societal support. This means that families are also economic relationships, in the sense that they are sites of work. Women tend to do a disproportionate amount of this reproductive labour – all the work that goes into maintaining people's lives and wellbeing, including cooking, cleaning, childcare, and attending to people's emotional needs. Men in heterosexual relationships, meanwhile, benefit from this work both because they tend to receive more care than they give, and because the responsibility for caring for others falls to their partner, which means that men themselves have more time for leisure and waged work.

Michèle Barrett and Mary McIntosh argue that family has become the principal site of care within capitalist society by outcompeting other possible social relations that could provide care. They write:

> The world around the family is not a pre-existing harsh climate against which the family offers protection and warmth. It is as if the family had drawn comfort and security into itself and left the outside world bereft. As a bastion against a bleak society it has made that society bleak. It is indeed a major agency for caring, but in monopolising care it has made it harder to undertake other forms of care.[1]

The family, then, has established a near-monopoly on care. Even when we pay for reproductive services such as childcare or eldercare, the responsibility for organising these services tends to fall on family members. This leads to a society where there is a distinct lack of care in all social spheres other than the family and some state institutions. Those who don't have any family ties are typically left with very minimal forms of support – if any – which sometimes is not enough to keep them alive.

In response to this enormous pressure on families and the care-lessness of society as a whole, feminists have suggested that the family should be abolished[2] While this might seem counterintuitive – a taking away of the only form of care people have access to – it is in fact a programme that seeks to redistribute caring work in ways that are less exploitative, violent, and exclusionary. It would also minimise the time we spend on reproductive labour, since the private household is an incredibly labour-intensive institution. It takes a lot more work for one person in every family or small household to cook food for a few people every day than it would take for a small group to cook for a hundred people. If a lot of the work that the family provides could be collectivised, then, we would not only be less reliant on the labour of a few people, but on a societal level we would be doing way less work to keep ourselves alive and well. That is time that could be better spent on leisure, creative pursuits, and general human flourishing.

Family abolition, then, does not mean the forcible separation of family members from one another. Instead it means spreading the work that families are currently doing, so that we would all have access to more caring relationships. Care would no longer be restricted to domestic and institutional settings. Instead, we could organise our lives so that better forms of care suffused society as a whole. But this requires not only prioritising the remaking of our social relationships within a broader anti-capitalist struggle, but also creating the infrastructures necessary to make life-sustaining practices available outside of the home.

Currently, domestic architecture is modelled on the labour- and resource-intensive one-family residence. Even though a lot of people don't live in traditional nuclear families, a dwelling typically has two or three bedrooms, a kitchen, one or two bathrooms, and a living room. This type of home is not necessarily appropriate for those who don't live in a family unit of two adults and between one and three dependent children. In the mid-twentieth century, there was some acknowledgement in the UK that housing needs to be 'mixed' to meet the needs of a broad range of people and household constellations.[3] Yet a lot of housing still seems to presuppose a small family, and all of it presupposes a household that does the bulk of its reproductive labour at home.

The problems with this model are particularly apparent when we look at housing provision for groups that aren't part of a nuclear family. Elderly people, especially single older people without much family support, often struggle to find housing and care provision that adequately meet their needs for accessibility and comfort. As Mike Berry writes, 'housing for the "old old" is in countries like my own, more of a "set and forget" option than a viable and effective stage in one's housing career. They are, in effect, filing cabinets for people past their usefulness in the productive labour force.'[4]

It's often hard to imagine something beyond this state of things. We seem to lack the ability to think beyond the private domestic household, as if this is simply a natural and non-political way of organising our living space. Helen Hester calls this failure to imagine anything other than the private nuclear household dwelling 'domestic realism', which she describes as

> the phenomenon by which the isolated and individualized small dwelling (and the concomitant privatization of household labor) becomes so accepted and commonplace that it is nearly impossible to imagine life being organized in any other way. That this occurs despite many people's lived experiences of the pressures and difficulties attendant

> upon reproductive labour as it is currently organized only serves to make it more remarkable.[5]

To Hester's concept of domestic realism (the sense that there are no alternatives to current forms of housing), we can add a complementary term – domestic romance (a sense that private domesticity is seen as desirable and good). Not only is the form of the domestic sphere taken for granted, it is also continually romanticised in our culture. Home is supposedly how we express a true sense of our selves, and having a beautiful and safe home is a central part of ideals of a good life more broadly. It is very hard to politicise home and its design, partly because of the sentimental attachment we have to the idea of private domesticity. Home, as Sam Johnson-Schlee writes, is a site of both isolation and attachment.[6] This makes it particularly fertile ground for emotion and desire, as it becomes the sphere most associated with flight from the world of work and competition outside the home. This also makes the home very easy to depoliticise, as it comes to appear to be the space of pure individuality and intimacy rather than connected to society more broadly.

Domestic realism and romance are not naturally occurring phenomena, but have been carefully created through cultural production and advertising. As I have argued, the single-family home is the commodity *par excellence*, which can in turn be filled with other commodities. One-family houses with gardens can typically be sold for more money than a flat. Taking care of a house and a garden not only takes a lot of work, but requires regular investment in other goods and services to make it nice. Not only capitalists themselves but also politicians have been involved in the production of domestic romance. In early and mid-twentieth-century US, there was a political decision to prioritise the development of suburban single-family dwellings over other forms of housing. This was also a way of establishing a more orderly working class, as white male workers were given access to mortgages and thus given a material and ideological stake in American capitalist society.[7] The model of suburban housing has since then been exported to other parts of the world, as part of American foreign policy and a weapon in the struggle against communism.[8] While it has not been uniformly adapted everywhere, it retains much of its romance as a symbol of a good life. As Alison Blunt and Robyn Dowling write, this American ideal of home and its manifestation in the form of a suburban one-family house have successfully been made transnational, as gated communities and 'Orange County style' homes are produced across the world.[9]

These types of home are not only labour-intensive, but resource-intensive as well. They are typically filled by individually owned and energy-intensive domestic appliances, and they are based on a culture of individual car ownership. They take up a lot of space, and large suburban gardens and lawns harm ecological systems and require inefficient use of water. This energy-inefficient model of housing was actively promoted by the advertising and cultural industries in the course of the twentieth century.[10] While there is an increasing social awareness of the impact of human activity on the climate, there hasn't yet been a radical break from the energy-inefficient one-family home as the standard model of housing provision.

Domestic realism and romance seem so integrated in current thinking about housing that neither the housing movement nor mainstream feminism has spent much time thinking about how housing could be redesigned to minimise the burden of domestic labour. Dolores Hayden writes that the feminist movement of the 1970s was mainly interested in redistributing labour within the heterosexual couple, pushing men to do their 'fair share', rather than rethinking the domestic sphere and its labours as such.[11] This tendency has remained in most feminist thinking, as there has been a lot written about the burden of domestic labour on women, but rarely any solutions offered beyond making men take on more of it, or paying people to do it. But the aim should be not just to redistribute this work, but to minimise it.

Hayden's seminal work traces an alternative feminist tradition – one that has sought to challenge domestic labour and domestic design. Her book *The Grand Domestic Revolution* outlines a history of American writers and activists who – at the height of bourgeois domesticity from the nineteenth to the early twentieth century – sought to resist domestic realism. This diverse tradition includes home economists, novelists, architects, housewives, city planners, and political organisers. There was never much consensus on exactly how domestic space and labour should be redesigned and rethought. Many of these early thinkers wanted domestic labour to be taken out of the home and to be professionalised – done for a wage by cooks, childminders, and cleaners, rather than performed for free by housewives in their isolated homes. But a more radical strand of thought suggested that people could create communities in which domestic work is shared. This, combined with redesigned living spaces and technology that would minimise the burden of domestic labour, would mean less work for most people – in particular the women who are still tasked with the lion's share of this work.

The new homes envisioned by this tradition were rarely built, because of a lack of money and resources. Planning law in the US also favoured single-family dwellings and more traditional apartment blocks.[12] But their designs were innovative, playful, and often technologically daring. In 1916, self-taught architect Alice Austin developed plans for a socialist and feminist city in Llano del Rio, California, in which labour-saving technology in communal kitchens and laundries, in combination with a sophisticated system of infrastructure, provided the basis for a city of kitchen-less homes where hot food was delivered to the house through a system of underground tunnels. Design features such as built-in furniture and heated floors instead of carpets sought to minimise the need for cleaning. While the community of Llano del Rio lacked the means to realise Austin's vision, her plans nonetheless opened up space beyond domestic realism.[13] Recognising that household technology in itself would do little to ease the burden of housework, especially as social standards for domestic cleanliness and childcare were continually being redefined, technology formed only a part of the strategy in feminist visions for a new domestic order, which ultimately sought to redefine social relations on a broad scale. The ideological and spatial separation of home, waged work, and leisure activities would be swept away.

Revitalising this tradition for the contemporary era, Helen Hester and Nick Srnicek call for a social world characterised by private sufficiency and public luxury, in which communal facilities such as swimming pools, libraries, cinemas, public transport, and so on would be located at the neighbourhood level and integrated in the domestic sphere.[14] And as facilities for leisure and transport could be merged with the domestic sphere from the outside, Hayden also points out that the caring work that currently happens in the private sphere could stretch out from the domestic space into the world.[15] Kitchens, laundries, childcare facilities, and support for elderly and disabled people could be located at a community level. This dual movement would cause a blurring of boundaries between the private and the public spheres.

While most thinkers within the movement for a redesigned society have recognised the need for people to have space to be alone, not all of our current domestic spaces are necessarily private. Currently, dominant domestic design rarely offers much privacy for members within the same family. As feminists have long recognised, mothers especially rarely have time or space to be alone in their homes, but are instead always on call, expected to be instantly ready to respond to family members' needs. A redesigned vision of the domestic sphere could ensure that some of those needs could be met elsewhere, and make space for mothers and others to be alone when they need it.

The main point of these projects, then, is to collectivise domestic labour. By making sure that much of the previously individualised work of reproducing ourselves is done collectively, it can also be minimised. Many hands make light work, especially if men are made to participate fully in currently feminised forms of labour. Collective forms of reproductive labour make it easier to ensure that everyone who can is contributing something, from each according to their ability, to each according to their need. The struggle to make men participate in domestic labour has often frustrated feminists on an individualised level. It is very difficult to do this in a privatised household, especially ones based around a heterosexual couple. Conflicts about domestic labour are a common contributing factor in relationship breakdown, which can leave women financially vulnerable and unable to secure adequate housing for themselves and their children. The loss of the relationship and the family as a whole might seem like too high a price to pay for a bit more equality. The dual-earner family form has been dominant since the 1970s in many parts of the world, and to some extent that forced men to 'help' with domestic chores, as their partners no longer had as much time for reproductive labour as a full-time housewife has. But it has been harder to make men take responsibility for domestic work as their own, not just something they are doing to help out. While some experiments in more collective forms of housing have tended to reproduce a gendered division of labour, in a collective setting, especially one where reproductive labour and care are core priorities, it might be easier to make men take full responsibility for traditionally feminised tasks.

In order to achieve this, collective housing needs to be explicitly paired with a feminist, queer project of family abolition. In early Soviet Russia, the move to collectivise housing was thought of as part and parcel of a move to create new forms of subjectivity, and also to move away from the bourgeois family form. However, the more utopian aspects of this project were quickly abandoned, and, with Stalin in power, the Soviet state was explicitly trying to re-establish the heterosexual nuclear family as a social ideal. A desperate housing shortage meant that often many families were packed into one apartment, so that the Soviets had to experience collective housing without abolishing the family or any sustained attempts to collectivise domestic labour. The results, unsurprisingly, were not great, and many people came to resent collective forms of housing.[16]

In place of this state-led push to abolish and then reintroduce the bourgeois family, contemporary family abolitionist thinkers emphasise offering people the collective resources and support needed to survive and even flourish, so that the family would no longer be an economic or social necessity. In her thinking on family abolition, M. E. O'Brien draws on the work of utopian socialist Charles Fourier, who planned phalansteries – a form of collective housing that would also provide spaces for communal reproductive labour and pleasure. Fourier imagined the phalanstery as a community of about 1,600 people, in custom-built housing that would provide both private rooms and shared spaces. Children would be reared communally. O'Brien adapts this vision to a contemporary model, and suggests that communities of 200 people would be more appropriate – big enough that reproductive labour and care could be carried out at a large scale, but small enough to encourage close ties between residents and democratic decision-making. This also means that existing domestic or commercial buildings could more readily be adapted, as many of them would provide enough space to house a couple of hundred people. She writes,

> Many things now done in the private home could be far better done in shared space: canteens can replace most kitchens and dining rooms; crèches replacing a child's individual play room; entertainment rooms could serve as

places to watch television or hang out in groups; personal studies could instead be shared libraries and co-working areas; home maintenance and cleaning equipment could be available in common space; vehicles could be similarly shared.[17]

In a similar vein to this reconfiguration of urban space, Hayden provides ideas for how existing suburban housing could be adapted to more communal models of care. What are currently one-family dwellings could be clustered so that some private houses, garages, and backyards are turned into communal space, with shared laundries, kitchens, daycare, and play areas, as well as space for shared gardening and leisure. Larger one-family homes could be redesigned to house more people.[18] In both of these visions, the idea is that reproductive labour is primarily provided by residents for themselves – either by taking turns to do different types of tasks, or by specialising according to individual preferences.

A core concern in these proposals is to provide domestic space that is more open to change, to different forms of domestic arrangements, and to enable individual choices beyond desires for the 'dream home' and its attendant forms of consumption and labour. As Barrett and McIntosh argue, creating material conditions for other forms of life, outside the normative family forms, is a way to start moving towards family abolition in the present.[19] This also means creating a range of different and adaptable forms of housing. An issue in contemporary housing is that if you have managed to achieve some degree of housing security, either by home-ownership or secure tenure, it's often quite difficult to move or to adapt your home so that it fits your needs. When housing choices are scarce, moving house might also mean that you end up far away from where you want to live. The imposition of the family as the dominant form of cohabitation implies that living with people who are not your romantic partner or in your family can be seen as a sign of failure, at least if you're no longer a young adult. Taken together, these pressures mean that people often live in homes that are too big, too small, or simply not suited to their household needs. It also means that they often stick with living with members of their families, even when those domestic relationships are not working very well, and sometimes avoid living with people who are not in their families, even when that would be beneficial. As Sophie K. Rosa writes, living with housemates is currently seen as a merely temporary arrangement, 'until partners, until property, until family, until settling down'.[20] But what if housemates were for life, not just for your twenties?

An aim of collectivising housing and reproductive labour, then, is to allow more flexibility both in terms of domestic design and in terms of cohabitation. In a commune like the one suggested by O'Brien, there would be plenty of space for people to move around within the commune, and there could be space adapted to a variety of different needs. More flexibility could literally be integrated into domestic space, as architects have developed moveable walls and attachable capsules that can be used to transform domestic space as the composition of the household and its needs change.[21] That would enable people to change their domestic space without having to move to a different place in the city or cut social ties with their neighbours and community. Having access to the care you need within the commune would also enable people to have more freedom over whether and with whom they want to cohabitate. A relationship breakdown would no longer mean a loss of financial, emotional, or physical security. This could make it easier for people to leave unsatisfactory relationships and find forms of cohabitation that would genuinely suit their needs, as well as enabling different forms of intimacy and pleasure. While communal housing has often been associated with an involuntary lack of privacy, it could be set up in such a way as to enable more genuine privacy *and* sociality, as it would not force us to share living space with others out of habit or economic necessity.

So how do we start changing our domestic space? O'Brien is sceptical of attempts to set up communes and co-ops under capitalism. She argues that the experiments of communal living that have been attempted have often included forms of withdrawal from capitalist society, attempting to create an 'outside' of capitalism while facing the pressures of existing within a capitalist economy and society. These attempts, she suggests, are doomed to fail. It is only with the overthrowing of the capitalist economy as a whole that we can meaningfully move towards building new forms of shared domesticity.[22] While I agree that co-ops and other forms of communal housing face a great deal of pressure, and currently rarely function as the communal form of housing that we need, I'm wary of totally dismissing attempts to build more communal housing in the present. There cannot be fully satisfactory forms of housing under capitalism. But waiting until moments of revolutionary change might imply that many people's needs will go unmet, and that we will miss an opportunity to start practising the collective self-management of housing and reproductive labour in the meantime.

While state-provided housing will necessarily form a part of solving the acute housing crisis in the UK today, especially by bringing down the cost of housing more broadly, we should not rely on the state to meet all our housing needs. As Karl Marx suggested in his writings on the Paris Commune, the bourgeois state has usurped many of the functions that people could fulfil for themselves, and the movement towards communism involves reclaiming power and capacities that properly belong to the people.[23] Part of the path towards undoing capitalism should thus involve undoing the state's grip on meeting our collective needs. Many people's needs have never been met adequately by the state, and for these groups in particular, self-managed collective housing might be an attractive option. The ingrained racism, ableism, heteronormativity, and sexism of the modern housing system might mean that self-management is more attractive to those groups who have historically and currently been excluded from state provision of housing, or given homes unsuited to their needs. While setting up forms of collective housing will take a lot of work, in the longer run it might feel worth it if labour can be minimised and more equally distributed within the communal home.

O'Brien's argument against communes in the present also hinges on an idea that the commune would necessarily attempt withdrawal from capitalist society. As Hester and Srnicek show in their overview of the history of communes, this has certainly often been the case. A romantic idea of withdrawal from society underpinned both the hippie communes of the late 1960s and the lesbian communes of the

1970s and 1980s. As these experiments in collective living often lacked money and resources, they were also forced to make do in inhospitable conditions. Rural communes offered very little material comfort and took a lot of work to run.[24] Yet there is nothing inevitable about the association of communal housing and withdrawal from society. Michael Harloe notes that social democratic states often rejected cooperative models of public housing, opting instead for models where housing was owned and managed by the state or charitable organisations. More cooperative models, he writes, are politically ambiguous, as they can easily slip into a model where communities are doing their best to manage their own hardship under capitalism, rather than pressuring the state to provide services. In this way, cooperative models can fit quite neatly into more conservative visions of society. But Harloe argues that this is why housing can't be taken as its own isolated aspect of life. In order to function well and actually start to challenge capitalist society, cooperative models of housing provision need to be one aspect within a broader culture and struggle for societal change. They must do more than just provide housing.[25] Similarly, Johanna Brenner argues for a model of cooperative housing that forms part of a broader movement for change.[26] Seen in this way, more collective forms of housing and reproductive labour could form the basis that allows revolutionary social change to happen.

The communes of the 1960s to the 1980s were often premised on an idea of a return to a more simple, rural life as an antidote to capitalist modernity, but we do not need to reject the city in favour of the countryside to start practising communal living, nor do we need to embrace a romanticised ideal of rural life. A core problem with urban communes is that land and housing in cities are often very expensive – way beyond what most people can afford. Favouring rural locations may therefore also be rooted in the very practical concern for costs. That also means that collective homeownership in cities, through co-ops or community land trusts, is not a viable strategy on its own. However, as part of a broader push to drive urban house prices down, it could form a valuable alternative to state-owned housing. There is a broader issue in terms of how to build feminist and communal housing, given our current lack of control over housing and land, and a shortage of resources and skills. But these issues can mainly be resolved through practice and experience, in dialogue with innovative thinking and design of space. Collective ownership allows a higher degree of control over housing, so that housing can be designed and built according to the needs of those residing in it. It might also allow for more radical solutions to the organisation of reproductive labour, which go beyond the piecemeal reforms imposed by the bourgeois state to support the smooth functioning of capitalist society. Hayden's practical suggestions for how to collectivise reproductive labour and housing involves setting up co-ops that use existing domestic space to provide shared reproductive resources in both urban and suburban environments.[27]

This aspect of collective control of housing is an attractive quality of co-ops and community land trusts. However, this does not exclude attempts to collectivise reproductive labour in rented accommodation. Because of the lower initial cost of renting, it will be preferable for many working-class people in cities. In fact, many people are already living in well-functioning shared housing in urban environments. This is mainly a side effect of the high cost of housing, but some people prefer sharing housing rather than living on their own, and may not desire traditional cohabitation through coupledom or family. In this way, the tensions within the capitalist economy, which privileges family structures but sometimes makes family life financially difficult to attain, have already provided a glimpse of what more communal forms of life could look like. When people are forced to share with strangers, this often leads to significant discomfort. But when people have the option of cohabiting with people they enjoy spending time with, shared housing can be both more joyful and less labour-intensive than households of one or two adults.

As Hester and Srnicek suggest, the state could also have a role in providing more communal housing.[28] This has in fact been the case in some social democratic projects, such as the Scandinavian countries and Vienna in the early twentieth century. These sought to create a more socialist and communal form of life through the provision of high-quality housing in conjunction with shared reproductive spaces for cooking, laundry, and childcare. While these plans were never fully realised, and typically continued to rely on sexist divisions of labour, they sought to embody some of the private sufficiency and public luxury that Hester and Srnicek call for.[29]

These different forms of housing could form part of a mixed set of tactics towards a housing system that is not only more affordable but better at meeting a broad range of our needs. This would be a housing movement that does not seek to opt out of capitalist society, but rather forms part of struggles for the remaking of society as a whole. The struggle for more collective housing cannot happen in isolation from other issues, because our need for housing is not separate from our needs for accessible healthcare, radical education, childcare, eldercare, better work conditions, a habitable planet, and joyful lives. We need affordable, collective housing so that we can better struggle for other things – so that we do not have to spend our lives between waged work and privatised unwaged work in the home. For those who do not have family, or whose families are far away or unable to care for them, having access to collective forms of care is especially essential. Blunt and Dowling write that cohousing might be particularly attractive for groups like elderly migrants, who need care and community but might not feel at home in society.[30]

A radical rethinking of our use of domestic space is also necessary in order to move away from our current path towards climate catastrophe. In the UK over the past few decades, individual use of domestic space has increased drastically, so that people now have much more space per person than they had only a generation ago. This implies a more inefficient use of domestic space, as well as more energy being required to light and heat more homes. There is a class aspect here as well, as wealthy families tend to have much more space, while proletarian households are more likely to live in overcrowded housing. In order to reduce the climate impact of housing, we need to cut the individual hoarding of domestic space.[31] In this way, family abolition is part of climate struggle.

There is no mechanical causality between space and sociality, so that more collective architecture automatically creates more communal social relations. But we can see the two as intertwined, so that more communal relationships create the need for more shared space. The spatial reconfiguration of life and reproductive labour therefore constitute an essential part of remaking the world beyond capitalism. To end the privatisation and care scarcity that currently blight our lives, we need the radical vision of family abolition and communal care. This means rejecting the domestic realism and romance that currently dominate much of the left, and instead starting to produce new visions of what communal life and labour could look like.

Conclusion

Organising Feeling, Transforming Home

I have been active in London's housing movement for several years now. Here, feelings are everywhere. Because home is such an intimate thing, how we feel about our housing can become the dominant feeling in our lives. People spend a lot of time at home, and if those homes are unsafe, or if you know that you might be made homeless, that will take a massive emotional toll and may make it impossible to think or feel about anything other than your housing situation. Housing movement spaces are very clearly emotional spaces – where people bring heavy or destructive feelings along with their housing issues. The support we offer has an emotional aspect which is sometimes more important than the practical support. We can give people knowledge about their rights, suggest steps they can take, or agree things we can do together to resolve their housing problems, but if those people do not feel that their housing situation could be different, or feel too scared or powerless to be able to take steps to change the situation, all the support we offer is meaningless.

Feeling is political. How we feel is not an internal truth of the individual self, but shaped through social processes. This means that political organisations and movements can do things with feelings. They can be built on and create feelings of anger, pity, jealousy, joy. Feelings can mobilise people, motivate them to take action. And equally, our social movements, unions, and groups have distinct feelings or moods. Sometimes we refer to this as 'vibe'. If we're more serious, we might say 'organisational culture'. But these are just different ways of naming that elusive sense of how an organisation feels, or, more precisely, how it *does* feeling. The term vibe is a way of naming a collective feeling, which doesn't have any single point of origin. Often we don't think about how we do (create, nurture, encourage, or discourage) feeling. But we all do it, with more or less attention to how our actions create and sustain particular moods and how those moods will impact others.

Doing feeling is a skill. Or rather, doing feeling well, in a way that takes into account how other people may interact with the feelings we create, takes a lot of time, energy, thoughtfulness, and practice. Setting the right emotional tone for a meeting, protest, or campaign might be the difference between success or failure, but often it's quite hard to capture and explain exactly how to do this. How do we create moments of shared anger against those in power? How do we create spaces that are emotionally nurturing and supportive? How do we encourage collective joy? How do we make sure our organising efforts are not derailed by jealousy and competition? I don't have many easy answers to these questions, but I want to stress that feeling is a key organising skill, and our movements rarely succeed unless we pay attention to how participants feel. By centring emotion, we can build organisations and movements that are more resilient, creative, and joyful. We can also start thinking of feeling as a tool we can mobilise to reach particular goals.

Sometimes there is an assumption that organising on the left is characterised by rifts and insoluble conflicts. There is also an expectation that most political groups will have a lifespan of just a few years. After that, they are either torn apart by conflict, or a sort of atrophy sets in and the group loses momentum. These collective emotional states are real. There are sometimes moments when it might be better for a group to split or cease to exist rather than spending all its time and energy working through conflict, and at times there isn't enough momentum or excitement to keep a collective project going. It might be that the original conditions that the group was created to respond to have changed. Or some key people have left and others are not capable of carrying the struggle forward. It's often quite hard to pinpoint exactly where these feelings come from. They don't necessarily stem from a single event. Feelings spread out, and many little events come to be interpreted within this new emotional framework. But these circumstances are not inevitable. With enough attention to the emotional life of a group, we can deal with conflict and bring new emotional and political energy into our organisations.

This begins with recognising that all of our political efforts are related to spheres of life that hold intense emotional meaning for many people. Whether we organise around or against migration raids, workplace exploitation, access to healthcare, police violence, or something else, these areas will hold various emotional connotations. As we mobilise and organise, we can learn what those feelings are, and how to use them for radical purposes.

This also means that the housing movement needs people who are skilled and confident not only in housing law or planning protests, but also in holding other people's emotions. This is often heavy work, as we witness and partake in the feelings of comrades and strangers alike; all the anxiety, anger, and discomfort people feel about their housing. Sometimes these negative feelings, stemming from a deeply unjust housing system, can become misdirected and aimed at the very people who are doing their best to help. Because this is difficult work, we need to create spaces that are also sustaining and sustainable – otherwise those of us who are active in these movements will collapse under the weight of those feelings. We need to hold each other, and make room for our own feelings, in order to be able to carry the feelings of others.

Supporting people in distress is part of the key left commitment to care for more people than you have intimate or familial bonds with. In a way, being on the left means caring for more people than we can know, as our solidarity extends to strangers. If the image of the 'old' left consists of dreary white men who only like to talk and don't care about feelings, there has always been an alternative stream of left organising focused on mutual aid and emotional support. But if the range of our caring becomes infinite – if it is open to anyone who seeks it – it's very easy to start feeling wrung dry after a while, especially when you're not getting emotional support yourself. We therefore need to centre the importance of caring for those who care. We need to build our organisations around emotional sustenance – the stuff that keeps you coming back, that makes organising sustainable and sometimes even joyful.

We also need to pay attention to who is performing most of this work of attending to the feelings of others. Because feeling is often seen as a natural or spontaneous state, stemming from a person's character, it's very easy to see some people as naturally emotionally gifted, whereas some people are less responsive to the emotional needs of others. This divide is typically gendered – women are seen as good at doing feeling while men are not good at it. But men use feeling all the time, albeit often in a different way. And the understanding of men as inherently emotionally unskilled helps them get out of the responsibility of attending to the emotional needs of other people. They are therefore freed from the obligation of dealing with emotion, and do so only when it suits them. This arrangement is self-reproducing, in that those who aren't socially obligated to work through to difficult feelings will not develop the skills necessary to do so. Doing feeling well takes practice. When we arrange our organisations around perceptions of what people are 'naturally' good at, we risk reproducing a system in which women are disproportionately made responsible for attending to the collective feeling of the group. Seeing feeling as a skill, and therefore also as something that can be learnt, is a way of undoing some of these gendered divisions of labour. It becomes the responsibility of men to train themselves in being attentive to the emotional needs of others.

But how organisations feel is itself only one part of the emotional aspects of the housing movement. We also use feeling when we talk about what housing should be. It's quite easy to draw on a bourgeois imaginary of emotional intimacy when talking about what home *should feel like*. Because home in bourgeois culture is represented as private and therefore non-political, housing movements risk slipping into an imaginary where housing is currently political, but the goal should be to depoliticise it and make it into the private space it ideally should be. If we're not careful, we might end up romanticising home and privatising feeling. In this vision of the home, it is seen as a place which should always feel secure and comforting, and the goal is to re-establish these feelings for those who currently don't experience them. But for many people, the bourgeois notion of home, and its attendant vision of private family life, will never be an option, nor do they necessarily desire it. Political discourses that privilege the feeling of security may also privilege home-ownership as the ideal form of tenure, as the opposite of the feelings of precarity and anxiety associated with being a private renter or being homeless. The feeling of security is also associated with being able to control space and limit who enters it – being able to exclude strangers and unwanted others, in favour of family members. Home, in this emotional imaginary, becomes conflated with the exclusive zone of private property and family life.

In order to avoid reinforcing a particular set of normative emotions, which in turn affirm bourgeois notions of property ownership and the separation between public and private, it's important that we also attach new emotional meanings to the notion of home. Home can be understood as an inherently political space, where notions of gender, sexuality, race, class, and labour are produced and reproduced.

While everyone should have access to feelings of safety, there is nothing that should make this feeling particular to the sphere of the home. And home could also be a space of collectivity, creativity, and joy, rather than just feelings of security and privacy.

We can also do more to sit with the bad feelings that home and housing issues currently create. Many people experience their housing situation as a central source of distress and anxiety in their lives. There are also many who experience a sense of shame in relation to their housing issues, as if their inability to access good-quality, affordable, and long-term housing is an individual failure rather than a system-wide condition. Inability to secure what our culture values the most – homeownership, normative family life, and a stable income – becomes felt as an individual shortcoming. Feelings of isolation are widespread, because we live in a culture which insists that we must all resolve our problems ourselves.

In contrast, struggles over housing can often challenge not only practical problems, but also the emotional states associated with housing precarity. As Paul Watt notes, there can be massive psychological gains from engaging in struggle with others, as such struggle can begin to break feelings of isolation and powerlessness.[1] Some of the most powerful moments of solidarity and care that I have witnessed involved turning feelings of anxiety and shame into anger – a feeling which places the source of the problem in the world, rather than in the individual. Anger is a way of expressing that the current state of things is unacceptable, and what we don't deserve what happens to us. It is a feeling that can be used to reveal rather than obscure social conflict. This use of feeling is not about turning negative feelings into more positive ones, but rather relocating the source of the bad feeling. A productive use of feeling for social movement is to turn anger into something that attaches to its proper object, and goes to the root of the problem. While anger is far from inherently radical, and has often been used for reactionary ends, it is a deeply social feeling. We can share anger. We can direct it at our real enemies – the government, bosses, landlords, police. The trick is to create a productive form of bad feeling that doesn't wear us down but acts as a driving force to keep us going. There can be a certain comfort, even joy, in feeling angry together with others.

As well as an emphasis on care and mutual support, then, we need movements that can create feelings of anger and antagonism. In protesting against letting agents, landlords, and politicians, I have found moments when we have released our shared sense of being exploited and ignored. In making our enemies fear us, in witnessing their discomfort, we can also glimpse a reversal of power dynamics and get to experience our own collective power. These moments of anger and joy intermingled are essential. The collective elation that comes from a successful protest or campaign – the feeling of having won, even if the victory is small – is what gives our struggle purpose. When we feel our power, we experience the rush of not only trying to compensate for one another's hurt, but actually pushing for a different political and emotional horizon altogether.

Bad feelings are an inherent part of political life. Sometimes the source of bad feeling is the organisation itself. Coming together with others is often a source of joy and solidarity, but trying to square our individual needs, desires, and opinions with those of many others is bound to create some discomfort. Conflict should not in itself be a reason not to try to do things together, but when not dealt with properly, feelings of discomfort and distress can become too much to hold. Sometimes we need to give ourselves the option of walking away from projects that are no longer emotionally sustainable. But we can also train ourselves in dealing with conflict in better ways. This means not trying to cover over the source of the hurt, but trying to get to the root of it. Dealing with conflict properly takes time and patience, but it's essential if we want to create organisations and movements that don't fall apart or have people leave as soon as someone's feelings are hurt.

Because we will get hurt. It wouldn't be realistic to expect our organisations, or any deeply personal relationships for that matter, to only be a source of good feeling. While we try to foster organisations that feel good to be part of, we also need to be prepared to deal with the bad feelings when they do arise. There have been moments when I've felt reluctant to carry on organising, but the emotional skill and attention of my comrades have pulled me through. Sometimes just listening to others expressing their feelings is the best thing we can do to support one another to keep being actively involved in struggle. A skilful use of emotion can change the feeling expressed through that very interaction, and turn it into something more collective and easier to bear. Shared feeling is essential for a sense of collectivity, of doing things together. This doesn't mean we can't challenge expressions of feeling that are misdirected, inappropriate, or destructive to our organisations. But we need to pay attention to these feelings, and do something with them, rather than simply ignoring them and hoping they will go away or magically become aligned with the feelings of the collective. Shutting down feeling, or accusing others of being emotional and therefore not rational, is not a way to deal with conflict.

There are those who demand a sanitised version of politics, in which we interact in ways that are formal and dictated only by the rules of the organisation. But we always interact with politics as whole individuals, messy emotions included. Arguing that an ideal political organisation is one where we discuss matters rationally and have only formal and non-personal interactions with one another is not only to adopt a bourgeois notion of subjectivity, in which feelings are appropriate in the private sphere only. It is also to set an unrealistic standard for what politics is, and one that is bound to fail as soon as feelings inevitably make themselves known. If our political organisations don't take steps to address our emotional needs, they are likely to only satisfy those who can adopt a bourgeois separation of the self, and those who can access emotional comfort elsewhere. In the essay 'Ecstasy and warmth', Automnia beautifully describes a different ideal of politics, in which our emotional needs for joy and comfort are not seen as separate from our lives as political agents. In fact, our political organisations can be a way of working through shared trauma and the misery of living under capitalism, as well as a source of emotional comfort and joy.[2] Especially when our emotional needs are created by the organisation itself, for instance when conflict or the work of supporting others creates strain on participants, it is also the role of the organisation to address those feelings and create political spaces that are emotionally satisfying and nourishing.

By thinking through comradeship as an emotional form, not only an intellectual or political affinity, we can begin to address the politics of intimacy and the intimacy of politics. Comrades can often provide emotional sustenance for those excluded from more conventional forms of intimacy, and also create emotional support that is pertinent to the struggles we engage in. The structures of emotional support we create should accurately reflect both the individual needs of participants and the content of our collective struggle. When successful, this form of intimacy can offer us a glimpse of a different world and a sense that our emotional needs and their satisfaction could look very different. Groups that are good at doing feeling thus not only become more enduring, but also show participants that the current social and emotional structures are not inevitable. We could develop forms of intimacy and emotional sustenance that are open and expansive rather than exclusive to a small group of people.

One of the best portrayals of this radical emotional potential of political activity is Robin Campillo's 2017 film *120 BPM*. Set in the early 1990s in Paris, it follows a group of people variously affected by the AIDS crisis as they form new kinds of intimacy, across conventional social borders. While there is nothing idealised in this portrayal, and the film also shows how hierarchy tends to sneak in and reproduce even in the most radical movements, *120 BPM* captures something important about the emotional life of a collective formed around a shared sense of anger and grief. It's about the petty conflicts that inevitably arise in politics, especially when people try to position themselves as the most radical, the most anti-capitalist. It's about the boredom we experience in meetings that go on forever. But it's also about shared moments of ecstasy, in the middle of all the destruction of which we have made ourselves the witnesses. The film posits dancing, sex, friendship, and other forms of intimacy as core parts of a political movement. It also captures the interplay of individual and collective feelings as the story shifts focus from the group, to a couple within the group, and then back to the collective. *120 BPM* shows a politics equally centred on intellectual and passionate political debates and protest and dancing as ways of being a body among other bodies. There are moments of failure to engage with others, bodies that shrink from each other, becoming a spectator rather than a participant, and the feeling of being outside of an emotional community. But even as individuals drift in and out of it, the collective has a certain consistency over time, and can welcome people back.

How do we create this sense of collectivity and shared feeling without becoming a clique, or without replacing one exclusive form of intimacy with another? I think the answer lies somewhere in this openness of feeling, where we are prepared to work through difference and conflict together. When we welcome people from different backgrounds and social positions into our movements, we make the emotional sustenance these groups offer available to an ever-wider set of people. We can achieve this by building relationships with new people as they join our groups, offering them new things to do, and also offering them the emotional support they need to do work that is often very different from what they have done before. Emphasising politics as a way of doing feeling, as an intimate yet expansive act, does not have to mean we should only organise harmoniously with people who are like ourselves. We don't have to agree on everything.

We don't always have to like each other. But we have to foster emotional attachment to the struggle itself, and to the collectives that struggle creates.

This book has explored some of the ways in which housing is tied up with the reproduction of capitalist social relations and forms of labour. Through notions of home, domesticity, and ownership, the housing system as we know it is an essential aspect of capitalist economies and modes of social reproduction. Not only is the ideal of homeownership, and especially the one-family home, deeply imbricated in the reproduction of normative family values, but home is also a space where generational and daily reproduction of labour power takes place. It is a space where many people experience exploitation and violence. It is a space where many people – especially those partly or fully excluded from capitalist labour markets – suffer from the harmful effects of substandard housing.

Rather than affirming the notion of 'home' as an unqualified good thing, which merely needs to be extended to everyone currently excluded from it, the housing movement could explore what home is under capitalist, sexist, racist, and ableist conditions, and how it needs to be transformed. This means interrogating our own tendencies for domestic realism and romance. The ideal of home is deeply ingrained in most people's psyches, so this is not an easy task. While many people on the left are critical of the Anglo-American obsession with homeownership (and particularly with the ownership of one-family houses with private gardens), it is often difficult to not desire the security that homeownership promises. But we need to continually challenge the social construction of home as only a space of safety and love, which is (or at least should be) non-political. I have heard people in the housing movement insist that home is and should be a private space. But unless we can both politicise home and deprivatise it, what are we even doing? Unless we can start chipping away at the bourgeois notion that home should be a sanctuary from politics, we will end up with a politics merely capable of reaffirming capitalist forms of social reproduction, rather than building a genuinely anti-capitalist movement.

This will involve reckoning with the emotional aspects of home. As we have seen, it is through homeownership and its relation to family and inheritance that many people gain a stake in the capitalist system, and in particular the current system of asset-based welfare and ever-increasing house prices. So when we say we want housing to be homes, not assets, we need to recognise that the two are currently intertwined. Many of the things we associate with home, such as security and family, are also ideas that shore up the ideal of homeownership. This means that we need to push for forms of safety that do not rely on ownership, but we also need to think of ways in which the affective ideal of security itself needs to be rethought. We need to interrogate how capitalist social relations are built into domestic architecture, and how they can be transformed. We shouldn't seek to build council housing that seeks to imitate the bourgeois ideals of privacy and defensible space. There are already too many homes designed for one family, with their own little front and back gardens. What we need is more space that can be part of transforming the social and emotional attachments we have to capitalist social reproduction.

Anti-capitalist movements strive for a different society not only through their demands and campaigns, but also through the way that they can start to build different types of sociality. These relationships are based on comradeship and solidarity – of a coming together across social difference to build a new world not based on the assumption that care only happens in intimate settings. An important part of any struggle is to start to transform the social relations of capitalism. While this work can't be completed under capitalism, as it depends on a wider transformation of material structures, the process of transformation needs to happen in conjunction with the struggle to change the economic and political structure. This means that we need to build structures of collective care, as well as practices that enable shared experiences of anger and joy, within our organisations. It is by creating the conditions for collective transformation that we can build a housing movement that is strong enough to fundamentally challenge capitalist structures of ownership.

If the housing movement keeps growing more powerful, we will also be increasingly able to set the agenda ourselves, rather than just reacting to government policies. The demands for an end to no-fault evictions, for rent controls, and for better housing conditions are all essential. But they are just the beginning. If we want to transform the housing system, we need to fight for more than just safe and affordable homes, as important as they are for our survival and wellbeing under capitalism. A powerful housing movement would be able to articulate *what we want*, rather than just what we're against. A vision for a housing system that can not only keep us safe but also fundamentally transform the way we live will become increasingly important.

As I have argued in this book, housing is a fundamental part of social reproduction. That also means that housing will be a key piece in the transformation of social reproduction and the way we live our lives. Through creating visions for a housing system that is collective rather than privatised, and able to undo the sharp distinctions between public and private, we can start the hard work of building a new world. Part of politicising housing involves breaking the sense of isolation, shame, and fear that characterises many people's current experience of home. In this more collective spirit, we can dream of housing that offers space for being together, space for being alone, space for rest, space for activities, democratic space for collective decision-making, space for care, and space for joy. We could start to build a desire for communism through struggle over reproduction and a life of less dependency on capitalism. As Sophie K. Rosa puts it, new forms of habitation 'could see the meaning of home transformed. A radical home is not secluded private property for a few bound by blood. It is a network of care; and embodiment of demands.'[3]

In this, we can start to imagine housing designs that suit varied needs, and particularly the needs of those who can't or won't live up to normative expectations of work and family life. There is already enough family-sized housing; let us demand more family-abolitionist-sized housing. We can centre the surplus, those at the margins of capitalist society, and ask what they want their housing to look like. We could create housing that is more responsive to changing household constellations, and more easily adaptive to the differing levels of physical ability that people might have over the course of a lifetime. We could find design solutions and technology that minimises domestic labour, and enables us to collectivise the labour that remains, rather than cementing expectations that reproductive work is an individual responsibility and a labour of love. We could ask questions such as: what kinds of housing would facilitate elderly and disabled people's need for both autonomy and care? What kinds of housing do those fleeing the nuclear family need? What kinds of housing would enable us to raise children together, outside of romantic coupledom? What kinds of housing would enable collective flourishing?

An analysis of the housing system that stops at a critique of current economic and legal structures does not enable us to ask these questions. While such a critique is essential, it tends to lead to a focus on the *form* of ownership of housing, rather than its content. The vision for the housing system we want thus tends to be left empty, and in this empty space, it's easy for naturalised and romantic assumptions about what 'home' is to sneak in. Unless we fill the housing struggle with new and radical visions for what housing could look like, the state and capital will likely seek to reintroduce normative family values and structures that enable capitalist forms of work. It's hard to combine the day-to-day grind of struggling for the bare minimum of housing security with these visions for a different future. But we will only have a chance of winning if we try.

Acknowledgements

Firstly, thanks to my editor, Rosie Warren, whose thoughtful work helped shape the early drafts of the book into something much better. And thanks to the Verso team for their work on this book and the previous one.

Helen Hester and Nick Bano kindly read the whole manuscript and provided helpful feedback and encouragement. Thanks also to Helen for her generous support of my work for almost a decade, and to Nick for being a patient listener when I needed to vent about the process of writing and editing this book.

The chapter 'No return to normal' was first published on the Greater Manchester Housing Action blog. Thanks to Isaac Rose for editing it.

This book was made possible by my own engagement in the housing movement. Thanks to my friends and comrades at London Renters Union – I owe you all so much. There are too many of you to name here, but this book wouldn't exist without you. Special thanks to Clare, Jacob, Kenny, and Michael, who got me involved when I was new and have remained some of my closest collaborators over the years.

Thanks to my friends who have encouraged and supported the development of this book, including Johanna, Pete, Isabell, Betty, Josh, Sophie, and Linn. And thanks to my family for their love and support – Catharina, Vide, Adam, and Esme.

Finally, I'm grateful to Dave, Jess, Martin, and Pixie, for making a home with me during the years I was working on this book.

Notes

Introduction: Housing Matters

1. Gráinne Cuffe, 'Number of first-time rough sleepers in London surges by 29%', *Inside Housing*, 31 January 2023.
2. Joe Beswick et al., 'Speculating on London's housing future', *City*, 20:2, 2016, pp. 321–41; Hettie O'Brien, 'The Blackstone Rebellion', *Guardian*, 29 September 2022.
3. Department for Levelling Up, Housing and Communities, *English Housing Survey: Headline Report 2022–2023*, p. 5; Department for Levelling Up, Housing and Communities, *English Private Landlord Survey 2021: Main Report*, p. 5.
4. Department for Levelling Up, Housing and Communities, *English Housing Survey: Headline Report 2022–2023*, p. 5.
5. Tom Slater, *Shaking Up the City: Ignorance, Inequality, and the Urban Question*, University of California Press, 2021, p. 148ff.
6. Susanne Soederberg, *Urban Displacements: Governing Surplus and Survival in Global Capitalism*, Routledge, 2021, pp. 28f.

7. Nick Bano, *Against Landlords: How to Solve the Housing Crisis*, Verso, 2024, pp. 29ff.
8. See, for example, Danny Dorling, *All That Is Solid: How the Great Housing Disaster Defines Our Times, and What We Can Do about It*, Penguin, 2014; John Boughton, *Municipal Dreams: The Rise and Fall of Council Housing*, Verso, 2018.
9. Department for Levelling Up, Housing and Communities, *English Housing Survey: Headline Report 2022–2023*, pp. 2, 33; Office for National Statistics, *Housing, England and Wales: Census 2021* (statistical bulletin), 5 January 2023.
10. Becky Tunstall, 'Relative housing space inequality in England and Wales, and its recent rapid resurgence', *International Journal of Housing Policy*, 15:2, 2015. See also Bano, *Against Landlords*, for a fuller account of this argument.
11. In the UK, 'affordable' housing is let or sold at 80 per cent of the market rate, which means it is unaffordable to most working-class people.
12. Sophus O.S.E. zu Ermgassen et al., 'A home for all within planetary boundaries: Pathways for meeting England's housing needs without transgressing national climate and biodiversity goals', 2022, *Ecological Economics*, 201: 107562.
13. Brett Christophers, *Rentier Capitalism: Who Owns the Economy, and Who Pays for It?*, Verso, 2020, p. 336.
14. Friedrich Engels, *The Housing Question*, Foreign Languages Press, 2021, p. 14.
15. Christophers, *Rentier Capitalism*, p. xxiv.
16. Neil Gray, 'Spatial composition and the urbanization of capital', in Neil Gray (ed.), *Rent and Its Discontents: A Century of Housing Struggle*, Rowman & Littlefield, 2018, pp. 49–67, at p. 50.
17. Ibid., p. 62.

18. As Diane Di Prima famously states in her poem 'Revolutionary Letter #8': 'NO ONE WAY WORKS, it will take all of us/ shoving at the thing from all sides to bring it down.' *Revolutionary Letters*, Last Gasp, 2007, p. 21.
19. Søren Mau, *Mute Compulsion: A Marxist Theory of the Economic Power of Capital*, Verso, 2023, p. 129.
20. Marta Russell, *Capitalism and Disability: Selected Writings by Marta Russell*, Haymarket Books, 2019.
21. Beatrice Adler-Bolton and Artie Vierkant, *Health Communism*, Verso, 2022, p. xvi.
22. Alison Blunt and Robyn Dowling, *Home*, Routledge, 2006, p. 10.
23. Susan Fraiman, *Extreme Domesticity: A View from the Margins*, Columbia University Press, 2019, p. 3.
24. Dolores Hayden, *Redesigning the American Dream: Gender, Housing, and Family Life*, W. W. Norton, 1984, p. 120.
25. Matrix, *Making Space: Women and the Man Made Environment*, Verso, 2022, pp. 9f.

1. No Return to Normal

1. Sophie Lewis, 'Houses into homes', University of California Humanities Research Institute, 2020.

2. Housing Is a Feminist Issue

1. Hayden, *Redesigning the American Dream*, p. 148.
2. The New York Wages for Housework Committee, *A Woman's Home Is Not Her Castle*, in Silvia Federici and Arlen Austin (eds), *The New York Wages for Housework Committee 1972–1977: History, Theory and Documents*, Autonomedia, 2018, p. 64.
3. Ibid., p. 65.
4. Hayden, *Redesigning the American Dream*, pp. 121f.
5. Ibid., pp. 55f.

6. Melinda Cooper, *Family Values*, Zone Books, 2017, p. 157.
7. Sara Reis, 'A home of her own: Housing and women', Women's Budget Group, 2019, p. 4.
8. Isabelle Atkinson, 'Housing justice is gender justice', National Partnership for Women and Families, 2022.
9. United States Census Bureau, 'Census Bureau Releases New Estimates on America's Families and Living Arrangements', 2022; Office for National Statistics, 'Families and households in the UK', 2022.
10. Michèle Barrett and Mary McIntosh, *The Anti-Social Family*, Verso, 2015, p. 24.
11. Soederberg, *Urban Displacements*, p. 279.
12. Reis, 'A home of her own', p. 4.
13. The US Department of Housing and Urban Development, *The 2020 Annual Homeless Assessment Report to Congress*, 2020, p. 20.
14. Paul Watt, 'Gendering the right to housing in the city: Homeless female lone parents in post-Olympics, austerity East London', *Cities*, 76, 2018, p. 48.
15. Soederberg, *Urban Displacements*, p. 279.
16. M. E. O'Brien, *Family Abolition: Capitalism and the Communizing of Care*, Pluto Press, 2023, pp. 41f.
17. Mike Berry, *A Theory of Housing Provision under Capitalism*, Palgrave Macmillan, 2023, p. 129.
18. Isabella Mulholland, 'Abused twice: The "gatekeeping" of housing support for domestic abuse survivors in every London borough', Public Interest Law Centre, 2022.
19. Ellen Malos and Gill Hague, 'Women, housing, homelessness and domestic violence', *Women's Studies International Forum*, 20:3, 1997, pp. 397–410 pp. 398, 401.
20. I'm grateful to Nick Bano for emphasising this point. Personal correspondence, 12 February 2024.

21. Paul Watt, *Estate Regeneration and Its Discontents: Public Housing, Place and Inequality in London*, Bristol University Press, 2021, p. 162.
22. Watt, 'Gendering the right to housing in the city', p. 48.
23. Shabna Begum, *From Sylhet to Spitalfields: Bengali Squatters in 1970s East London*, Lawrence Wishart, 2023, pp. 67, 130.

3. *Never at Home*

1. David Madden and Peter Marcuse, *In Defense of Housing: The Politics of Crisis*, Verso, 2016, p. 68.
2. Department for Levelling Up, Housing and Communities, *English Housing Survey: Headline Report 2022–2023*, p. 34.
3. Nick Bano, 'Stepping up the housing struggle', *Tribune*, 22 June 2022.
4. Ash Sarkar, 'We asked landlords why they're making the cost-of-living crisis their tenants' problem', *Novara*, 24 August 2022.
5. Generation Rent, 'No-fault evictions drive up homelessness', 18 August 2018.
6. Shanti Das, 'Bidding wars, cash up-front and "auditions" – inside Britain's broken renting market', *Guardian*, 28 August 2022.
7. Madden and Marcuse, *In Defense of Housing*, p. 55.
8. Trust for London, 'Rent for a one-bedroom dwelling as a percentage of gross pay by London borough (October 2022 to September 2023)', 2023.
9. Ruth Wilson Gilmore, *Abolition Geography: Essays Towards Liberation*, Verso, 2022, pp. 12f.
10. Statista, 'Government expenditure on housing benefit in nominal terms in the United Kingdom from 2000/01 to 2020/21', 1 April 2022.

11. David Frost, 'The Tory assault on buy-to-let is another step on the road to socialism', *Telegraph*, 17 June 2022; Bano, *Against Landlords*, pp. 2ff.
12. Ibid., p. 106.

4. *Poor Housing Creates Poor Health*

1. Matthew Taylor, 'Failure to insulate UK homes costing thousands of lives a year, says report', *Guardian*, 13 March 2024.
2. Housing Ombudsman, 'Spotlight on damp and mould: It's not lifestyle', 26 October 2021.
3. Building Research Establishment, 'BRE report finds poor housing is costing NHS £1.4bn a year', 9 November 2021.
4. Nick Bano, 'The housing crisis is bad for your health', *Tribune*, 28 May 2021.
5. Russell, *Capitalism and Disability*, p. 3.
6. Adler-Bolton and Vierkant, *Health Communism*, p. 21.
7. Daniel Renwick and Robbie Shilliam, *Squalor*, Agenda Publishing, 2022, p. 56.
8. Slater, *Shaking Up the City*, p. 150.
9. Renwick and Shilliam, *Squalor*, p. 128.
10. Ibid., pp. 90, 117.
11. Katherine Swindells, 'A third of adults in Britain live in unsafe and insecure housing', *New Statesman*, 26 May 2021; Damien Gayle, 'People of colour far likelier to live in England's very high air pollution areas', *Guardian*, 4 October 2022.
12. Emiliano Mellino, '"It's almost the same as living on the street": This is how people picking your vegetables have to live', *The Bureau of Investigative Journalism*, 13 April 2023.
13. Lauren Berlant, 'Slow death (sovereignty, obesity, lateral agency)', *Critical Inquiry*, 33:4, 2007, pp. 754–80. See also Adler-Bolton and Vierkant, *Health Communism*, p. 1.

14. Adler-Bolton and Vierkant, *Health Communism*, p. 18; Renwick and Shilliam, *Squalor*, p. 111.
15. Peter Apps, *Show Me the Bodies: How We Let Grenfell Happen*, Oneworld Publications, 2022.
16. Friedrich Engels, *The Conditions of the Working Class in England*, Penguin, 2009, p. 127.
17. Ibid., p. 101.
18. Stuart Hall and Bill Schwarz, 'State and society, 1880–1930', in Stuart Hall, *The Hard Road to Renewal*, Verso, 1988, pp. 95–122, at p. 96. See also Gilmore, *Abolition Geography*, pp. 210, 412.
19. Leopoldina Fortunati, *The Arcane of Reproduction: Housework, Prostitution, Labor and Capital*, Autonomedia, 1995, pp. 172ff.
20. Berlant, 'Slow death', p. 760, italics in original.
21. Apps, *Show Me the Bodies*, p. 296.
22. Stuart Hodkinson, *Safe as Houses: Private Greed, Political Negligence and Housing Policy after Grenfell*, Manchester University Press, 2019; Apps, *Show Me the Bodies*.
23. Robert Booth, 'Social landlord in England said mould was "acceptable" in refugees' homes', *Guardian*, 28 March 2023.
24. Adler-Bolton and Vierkant, *Health Communism*, p. 179.

5. *The Feeling of Ownership*

1. Secured by Design, 'About SBD', securedbydesign.com.
2. Cara Chellew, 'Defending suburbia', *Canadian Journal of Urban Research*, 28:1, 2019, pp. 19–33, at p. 23.
3. Sophie K. Rosa, *Radical Intimacy*, Pluto Press, 2023, p. 124.
4. Jane Jacobs, *The Death and Life of Great American Cities*, Pelican Books, 1965, pp. 199, 338, 351.
5. Oscar Newman, *Defensible Space*, Architectural Press, 1973, p. 3.
6. Ibid., p. xiv.

7. Alice Coleman, *Utopia on Trial: Vision and Reality in Planned Housing*, Hilary Shipman, 1985, p. 23.
8. Jacobs, *The Death and Life of Great American Cities*, pp. 44f., 73; Newman, *Defensible Space*, p. 27; Coleman, *Utopia on Trial*, p. 139.
9. Newman, *Defensible Space*, p. 19; Coleman, *Utopia on Trial*, pp. 18, 118.
10. Jacobs, *The Death and Life of Great American Cities*, pp. 31f.; Newman, *Defensible Space*, pp. 79, 100; Coleman, *Utopia on Trial*, pp. 19f.
11. Coleman, *Utopia on Trial*, p. 20.
12. Newman, *Defensible Space*, p. 3.
13. Jacobs, *The Death and Life of Great American Cities*, pp. 39f.
14. Newman, *Defensible Space*, pp. 203f.
15. Coleman, *Utopia on Trial*, p. 29; Renwick and Shilliam, *Squalor*, pp. 118f.
16. For detailed accounts of broken windows policing, see Christina Heatherton, Jordan T. Camp (eds), *Policing the Planet: Why the Policing Crisis Led to Black Lives Matter*, Verso, 2016.
17. Newman, *Defensible Space*, pp. 4ff., 207.
18. Ibid., p. 51.
19. Coleman, *Utopia on Trial*, pp. 18, 118.
20. Newman, *Defensible Space*, pp. 89ff.; Coleman, *Utopia on Trial*, p. 147.
21. Renwick and Shilliam, *Squalor*, p. 74.
22. Coleman, *Utopia on Trial*, p. 32.
23. Ibid., pp. 32, 178.
24. Newman, *Defensible Space*, p. 79.
25. Angus Johnston, 'Don't look now', *New Inquiry*, 2014.
26. Coleman, *Utopia on Trial*, pp. 86, 184.
27. Ibid., p. 10.
28. Newman, *Defensible Space*, pp. 189, 191.

29. Coleman, *Utopia on Trial*, p. 87.
30. Blunt and Dowling, *Home*, p. 115.
31. Coleman, *Utopia on Trial*, p. 87.
32. Jacobs, *The Death and Life of Great American Cities*, p. 412; Newman, *Defensible Space*, pp. 203f.; Coleman, *Utopia on Trial*, p. 161.
33. Nye Bevan, quoted in Boughton, *Municipal Dreams*, p. 97.
34. Blunt and Dowling, *Home*, p. 171.
35. Coleman, *Utopia on Trial*, pp. 46, 102.
36. Ibid., p. 171.
37. Lynsey Hanley, *Estates: An Intimate History*, Granta, 2012, pp. 104, 216ff.
38. Zoe Hu, 'The agoraphobic fantasy of tradlife', *Dissent*, 70:1, 2023, pp. 54–9.
39. Coleman, *Utopia on Trial*, p. 177.
40. Boughton, *Municipal Dreams*, p. 184.
41. R. I. Mawby, 'Defensible space: A theoretical and empirical appraisal', *Urban Studies*, 14:2, 1977, pp. 169–79.
42. Thanks to Nick Bano for making this point. Personal correspondence, 12 February 2024.
43. Coleman, *Utopia on Trial*, p. 184.

6. *Inheriting the Family Home*

1. Marco Albertini, Marco Tosi, and Martin Tohli, 'Parents' housing careers and support for adult children across Europe', *Housing Studies*, 33:2, 2018, pp. 160–77, at p. 160.
2. See Bano, *Against Landlords*, for a detailed account of how private rents affect house prices.
3. Hayden, *Redesigning the American Dream*, p. 33.
4. Cited in Lorna Fox O'Mahony and Louise Overton, 'Asset-based welfare, equity release and the meaning of the owned home', *Housing Studies*, 30:3, 2015, pp. 392–412, at p. 394.

5. Lisa Adkins, Melinda Cooper, and Martijn Konings, *The Asset Economy: Property Ownership and the New Logic of Inequality*, Polity, 2020, p. 43.
6. Ibid., pp. 4ff.
7. Cooper, *Family Values*, pp. 144, 151.
8. Brett Christophers, 'Intergenerational inequality? Labour, capital, and housing through the ages', *Antipode*, 50:1, 2017, pp. 101–21, at p. 116.
9. Statista Research Department, 'Homeownership rate in the United States from 1990 to 2023', 2024; Department for Levelling Up, Housing and Communities, *English Housing Survey: Headline Report 2022–2023*, p. 5.
10. Christophers, 'Intergenerational inequality?', p. 101.
11. Cooper, *Family Values*, pp. 121, 162.
12. Rory Coulter, 'Parental background and housing outcomes in young adulthood', *Housing Studies*, 33:2, 2018, pp. 201–23, at p. 202.
13. Albertini, Tosi, and Kohli, 'Parents' housing careers and support for adult children across Europe', pp. 163f.
14. Ibid., p. 161.
15. Brett Christophers, 'A tale of two inequalities: Housing-wealth inequality and tenure inequality', *Environment and Planning A: Economy and Space*, 53:3, 2019, pp. 573–94, at pp. 578, 589; Peter Kemp, 'Private renting after the global financial crisis', *Housing Studies*, 30:4, 2015, pp. 601–20, at p. 612.
16. Adkins, Cooper, and Konings, *The Asset Economy*, p. 44.
17. Karl Marx and Friedrich Engels, *The Communist Manifesto*, Penguin, 2002, p. 239.
18. Lindsay Flynn and Herman Mark Schwartz, 'No exit: Social reproduction in an era of rising income inequality', *Politics and Society*, 45:4, 2017, pp. 471–503, at p. 472.

7. *Demanding More, Demanding Better*

1. Sophie Watson and Helen Austerberry, *Housing and Homelessness: A Feminist Perspective*, Routledge, 1986, p. 37.
2. Watt, *Estate Regeneration and Its Discontents*, p. 56.
3. Thomas Wainwright and Graham Manville, 'Financialization and the third sector: Innovation in social housing bond markets', *Environment and Planning A*, 49:4, 2016, pp. 819–38.
4. Hodkinson, *Safe as Houses*.
5. Joe Beswick and Joe Penny, 'Demolishing the present to sell off the future? The emergence of "financialized municipal entrepreneurialism" in London', *International Journal of Urban and Regional Research*, 42:4, 2008, pp. 612–32, at p. 625.
6. Watt, *Estate Regeneration and Its Discontents*, p. 88.
7. Michael Harloe, *The People's Home? Social Rented Housing in Europe and America*, John Wiley & Sons, 1995, pp. 17, 73, 511ff.
8. Madden and Marcuse, *In Defense of Housing*, p. 119.
9. Boughton, *Municipal Dreams*, p. 6.
10. Vicky Spratt, *Tenants*: *The People on the Frontline of Britain's Housing Emergency*, Profile Books, 2022, pp. 206ff.
11. Hodkinson, *Safe as Houses*, p. 23.
12. Sita Balani, *Deadly and Slick: Sexual Modernity and the Making of Race*, Verso, 2023, p. 62.
13. See, for example, Spratt, *Tenants*, pp. 29, 217.
14. Watt, *Estate Regeneration and Its Discontents*, pp. 43f.
15. Harloe, *The People's Home?*, p. 426.
16. Renwick and Shilliam, *Squalor*, pp. 46, 32.
17. Begum, *From Sylhet to Spitalfields*, p. 61.
18. Watt, *Estate Regeneration and Its Discontents*, p. 139.
19. Balani, *Deadly and Slick*, pp. 62, 66.
20. Robbie Shilliam, *Race and the Undeserving Poor: From Abolition to Brexit*, Columbia University Press, 2018, p. 92.

21. Begum, *From Sylhet to Spitalfields*, p. 50.
22. Adah Kaye, Marjorie Mayo, and Mike Thompson, 'Inner London's housing crisis', in John Cowley, Adah Kaye, Marjorie Mayo, and Mike Thompson (eds), *Community or Class Struggle?*, Stage 1, 1977, pp. 128–68, at p. 160.
23. Ibid., p. 148.
24. Watt, *Estate Regeneration and Its Discontents*, p. 201.
25. Harloe, *The People's Home?*, pp. 196, 269, 273.
26. Madden and Marcuse, *In Defense of Housing*, p. 128.
27. Harloe, *The People's Home?*, p. 443.
28. Eve Blau, *The Architecture of Red Vienna 1919–1934*, MIT Press, 1999, pp. 140, 226f.; Soederberg, *Urban Displacements*, p. 188.
29. Ibid., p. 26ff; see also Soederberg, *Urban Displacements*, p. 188.
30. Blau, *The Architecture of Red Vienna*, pp. 39f.
31. Ibid., pp. 38ff., 149f.
32. Soederberg, *Urban Displacements*, p. 182.
33. Blau, *The Architecture of Red Vienna*, p. 150.
34. Renwick and Shilliam, *Squalor*, p. 32.
35. Watson and Austerberry, *Housing and Homelessness*, pp. 11, 49.
36. Hayden, *Redesigning the American Dream*, p. 120.
37. Don Watson, *Squatting in Britain 1945–1955: Housing, Politics and Direct Action*, Merlin Press, 2016, p. 179.
38. Boughton, *Municipal Dreams*, p. 265.
39. Harloe, *The People's Home?*, pp. 3, 7, 536.

8. Collective Housing and the Abolition of the Family

1. Barrett and McIntosh, *The Anti-Social Family*, p. 80.
2. See particularly Sophie Lewis, *Abolish the Family: A Manifesto for Care and Liberation*, Verso, 2022; M. E. O'Brien, *Family Abolition*.
3. Boughton, *Municipal Dreams*, p. 102.
4. Berry, *A Theory of Housing Provision Under Capitalism*, p. 132.

5. Helen Hester, 'Promethean labors and domestic realism', *E-Flux*, September 2017.
6. Sam Johnson-Schlee, *Living Rooms*, Peninsula Press, 2022, p. 20.
7. Dolores Hayden, *The Grand Domestic Revolution: A History of Feminist Designs for American Homes, Neighborhoods, and Cities*, MIT Press, 1983, pp. 23, 283.
8. Helen Hester and Nick Srnicek, *After Work: A History of the Home and the Fight for Free Time*, Verso, 2023, pp. 136ff.
9. Blunt and Dowling, *Home*, pp. 243f.
10. Hayden, *Redesigning the American Dream*, p. 34.
11. Hayden, *The Grand Domestic Revolution*, p. 295.
12. Hester and Srnicek, *After Work*, p. 126.
13. Hayden, *The Grand Domestic Revolution*, pp. 242ff.
14. Hester and Srnicek, *After Work*, pp. 179ff.
15. Hayden, *The Grand Domestic Revolution*, p. 295.
16. Lynne Attwood, *Gender and Housing in Soviet Russia*, Manchester University Press, 2010, pp. 107ff.
17. M. E. O'Brien, 'Communizing care', *Pinko*, 15 October 2019.
18. Dolores Hayden, 'What would a non-sexist city be like? Speculations on housing, urban design, and human work', *Signs: Journal of Women in Culture and Society*, 1980, 5:3, S170–S187, at p. S186.
19. Barrett and McIntosh, *The Anti-Social Family*, p. 134.
20. Rosa, *Radical Intimacy*, p. 136.
21. Hayden, *Redesigning the American Dream*, p. 118.
22. O'Brien, 'Communizing care'.
23. Karl Marx, *The Political Writings*, Verso, 2019, p. 934.
24. Hester and Srnicek, *After Work*, pp. 140ff.
25. Harloe, *The People's Home?*, pp. 512ff.
26. Johanna Brenner, 'Democratizing care', 15 December 2017, versobooks.com.

27. Hayden, 'What would a non-sexist city be like?', pp. S181ff.
28. Hester and Srnicek, *After Work*, p. 178.
29. Ibid., pp. 126ff., 161ff.; see also Blau, *The Architecture of Red Vienna 1919–1934*.
30. Blunt and Dowling, *Home*, p. 265.
31. Sophus O.S.E. zu Ermgassen et al., 'A home for all within planetary boundaries'.

Conclusion: Organising Feeling, Transforming Home

1. Watt, *Estate Regeneration and Its Discontents*, p. 361.
2. Automnia, 'Ecstasy and Warmth', *The Occupied Times*, 21 August 2015.
3. Rosa, *Radical Intimacy*, p. 130.